Olfaction in Early Childhood Research and Practice

An innovative exploration into the immediate and profound effects of sensory engagement, this book delves specifically into the incorporation of smell within the context of contemporary childhood experiences. Thinking to future advancements in educational technology, it is expected that digital media will eventually integrate all senses. This book outlines the convergence of children's learning and olfaction, setting the groundwork for future-oriented early education that seamlessly integrates sensory learning with advancements in technology.

Guided by child development theories and recent insights into embodiment, socio-material theories and affective literacy, chapters explore:

- The opportunities of olfaction in early education research and practice
- Developing olfactory literacies
- Olfaction in children's reading and story-telling
- Cultural and socio-technical influences on olfaction
- Anticipating olfactory education futures

This unique book is the first volume to communicate the power of smell in early childhood, paving the way for new approaches that empower children through innovative multisensory experiences.

Natalia Ingebretsen Kucirkova is Professor of Early Childhood and Development, Norwegian Centre for Learning Environment, University of Stavanger, Norway, and Professor of Reading and Children's Development at The Open University, UK.

Olfaction in Early Childhood Research and Practice

How the Study of Smell Charts New Frontiers in Early Education

Natalia Ingebretsen Kucirkova

Routledge
Taylor & Francis Group
LONDON AND NEW YORK

First published 2025
by Routledge
4 Park Square, Milton Park, Abingdon, Oxon OX14 4RN

and by Routledge
605 Third Avenue, New York, NY 10158

Routledge is an imprint of the Taylor & Francis Group, an informa business

British Library Cataloguing-in-Publication Data
A catalogue record for this book is available from the British Library

ISBN: 978-1-003-48201-7 (hbk)
ISBN: 978-1-032-77247-9 (pbk)
ISBN: 978-1-003-48202-4 (ebk)

DOI: 10.4324/9781003482024

Typeset in Times New Roman
by Taylor & Francis Books

Contents

1 Introduction

Life is a fusion of sensory experiences, each playing a vital role in how we perceive and interact with the world. From the colours and images we see, to the sounds and tones we hear, and the textures we feel and taste – every sensation contributes to our understanding of our surroundings. However, when it comes to education, there seems to be a bias towards prioritizing sight and sound, relegating touch, smell, and taste to the sidelines. In this book, I aim to shed light on the often-overlooked sense of smell. By foregrounding smell, I hope to highlight the importance of *all* senses in learning and to raise awareness of the fascinating possibilities with this remarkable sense.

Adults typically nurture children's visual, auditory, and tactile senses through activities such as reading, exposure to music, and fine motor skill development, but the sense of smell, also referred to as "olfaction", often receives inadequate attention. Recognizing the profound impact that odours can have on cognitive processes and emotional well-being, there is a compelling need to integrate olfactory experiences more intentionally into early childhood education and everyday routines. By doing so, we can harness the rich potential of smell to positively influence children's behaviour and, through this pathway, possibly also influence their learning and overall sensory experiences.

Expressions related to the sense of smell are notably sparse within the English language. We rely heavily on a handful of terms such as "stink", "odour", "smell", "scent", and "fragrance" to articulate both positive and negative olfactory experiences. However, these descriptors are often broad and abstract, lacking the specificity required to precisely convey the nuances of various scents. What one individual perceives as a pleasant fragrance may be interpreted as an offensive stench by another. Consequently, the linguistic landscape surrounding smell appears elusive and challenging to navigate. To me, it highlights the underdeveloped relationship between language and olfaction; a

DOI: 10.4324/9781003482024-1

relationship that can be nurtured from a young age and improved over time. Indeed, the possibility to precisely name and describe different odours is something that I hope future generations of children will be better at than we are today.

Children possess a remarkably acute sense of smell, which plays a significant role in their daily routines and experiences. From potty training to bedtime rituals involving soothing balms, odours shape many aspects of children's lives. Smells have a unique ability to forge connections between experiences and events, and between sensation and time. Yet, the full potential of olfaction in influencing children's development and behaviour has largely been overlooked by research. Most studies in olfactory applications focus on adult-oriented marketing strategies, and the commercial value of adding smell for, for example, increasing consumers' shopping behaviours.

In this book, I draw upon research conducted with children in Global North and Global South countries, encompassing both conceptual investigations through literature reviews and empirical studies conducted in kindergartens. I also draw on some grey literature and direct experience of olfactory art. For the latter, I dipped my toes into the perfume industry by undertaking The Certificate in Perfumery Art course, meeting several olfactory artists and designers at networking events and conferences and discussing the implications of impoverished olfactory landscapes with urban professionals and olfactory experts. Through the diverse perspectives, learnings, and experiences I have collected for this book, I aim to illuminate the multifaceted significance of olfaction in childhood development and its many potential implications for education.

BJ Miller, a prominent figure in palliative care, eloquently articulated in his reflective TED Talk that what really matters at the end of life is our senses; our senses serve as vital conduits to what defines our humanity and fosters connection. Miller, having lost all four limbs, underscores the profound significance of retaining even a single sense, as it offers the potential to access that which makes us feel human and interconnected. This sentiment underscores why I emphasize the importance of engaging all the senses in learning experiences. Through our ability to feel, to perceive, we reaffirm our humanity and our connection to the world around us. By nurturing and celebrating the sense of smell alongside other senses, we honour the diverse ways individuals experience and interact with their environment. In doing so, we not only promote inclusivity but also deepen our understanding of what it means to be human and connected in an increasingly digitized world.

That said, I do not view olfactory or multisensory engagement as an antidote to digital engagement. Digital advancements will undoubtedly continue to shape the landscape of education. Currently, generative artificial intelligence (AI) dominates many discussions surrounding the future of learning, which to me highlights how much technological trends, rather than scientific trends, shape our projections for the future. True progress, in my opinion, lies in our ability to harness and enhance our sensory faculties, including smell, to navigate the world more effectively. Rather than viewing technology as a replacement for our senses, I believe in leveraging it to complement and amplify our sensory experiences. By strategically training our senses, particularly our olfactory sense, we can unlock new dimensions of perception, enabling us to engage with the world with greater sophistication and depth. In this context, a real educational advancement would not solely be in the proliferation of digital tools, but in our capacity to integrate sensory awareness into our daily lives and educational practices. By embracing a holistic approach that values both technological innovation and sensory exploration, we can cultivate a more nuanced understanding of learning futures.

About this book

This book draws on extensive research to offer an evidence-based perspective on the relationship between olfaction and children's learning development. The empirical basis for the book is a project that I have led over the past few years in Norway and Malawi. The project was the first of its kind to receive funding specifically focused on exploring the role of smell in children's learning and reading. Supported by the Norwegian Research Council and additional personal fellowships from the Jacobs Foundation and INVEST in Finland, the research aimed to delve into the uncharted territory of olfaction and young children's reading of print and digital books.

The project's exclusive focus on children and olfactory experiences in early childhood stemmed from two primary motivations. First, this area remains vastly underexplored in existing research, despite its undeniable significance. Early childhood is a critical period wherein foundational experiences are established and developed, making it an opportune time to investigate the role of smell in shaping cognitive and emotional development.

Second, delving into the relationship between olfaction and learning holds immense potential for the future of education. By exploring how olfactory experiences influence learning processes and outcomes, we can gain valuable insights into optimizing educational practices and enhancing student engagement. Thus, the work presented in this book not only addresses a notable gap in the current understanding of early childhood, but also aspires to lay the groundwork for transformative advancements in educational practice.

Multidisciplinary and multimethodological approaches

The work presented in this book, and pursued in our project, has relied on both qualitative and quantitative (mixed) methods as well as interdisciplinary perspectives on smell and early childhood education. As a collaborative endeavour, the project has drawn upon insights from not only researchers but also librarians, olfactory artists, and teachers and scientists representing various disciplines (psychology, education, human–computer interaction, literary studies, critical studies, neuroscience, marketing research, chemistry, and physics).

I purposefully combine various insights into an interdisciplinary approach with the goal of piecing together a comprehensive understanding of smell in childhood. Each perspective brings its own unique insights and methodologies to the table. The biological perspective, for example, delves into the intricate mechanisms underlying olfaction, exploring how sensory receptors detect and process odour molecules, and how these signals are transmitted and interpreted by the brain. The social sciences perspective approaches smell as a signifier and factor that influences human relationships. Yet another insight is offered by the critical literacy approach, which proved invaluable in a study where we aimed to document the ephemeral properties of smell that, while intangible, had a material influence on children's literacy experience.

So, while the individual studies summarized in this book may stem from various disciplines, resulting in separate and multidisciplinary perspectives, by synthesizing them in this book, I aim to foster an *interdisciplinary* understanding of the multifaceted interplay between olfaction and childhood development.

In the case of exploring new territory, the diversity of perspectives is important. However, this may not provide the same depth of understanding as a single-discipline perspective would offer. Readers interested in, for example, the chemical composition of smell and neuroscientific approaches, or readers interested in critical studies of smell's role in civic life, may find this book only scratching the surface of what merits a full volume. Nevertheless, I hope this book piques the curiosity of scholars across multiple disciplines, encouraging them to contextualize the content in their own work and continue the journey I have only initiated in this modest volume.

Basic properties of smell (the biological perspective)

Humans possess an extraordinary ability to distinguish between different odours. While early estimates suggested that humans could discern around 10,000 odours, recent research has proposed much higher numbers. One study indicated that we may be capable of distinguishing at least 1 trillion odours (Bushdid et al., 2014). However, further analysis has called this figure into question, as it varies significantly depending on the methodology used (Majid, 2021). While the exact number of odours that humans can distinguish is unknown, there is no doubt that humans can distinguish an extraordinary amount of smells, many more than we can name or describe in words.

The scarcity of replication studies in olfactory research highlights the challenges inherent in this emerging field. Namely, our current understanding relies heavily on individual studies rather than a robust body of research. It is therefore crucial to approach each study with caution, recognizing its tentative nature and understanding that the insights it offers may not be universally applicable. With this caveat in mind, several recent studies have provided valuable insights into the workings of the olfactory system. While these findings should be interpreted with the understanding of their limitations, they offer unique perspectives that contribute to our evolving understanding of olfaction in humans.

For example, a recent study published in the *Journal of Neuroscience* sheds new light on the complexity of the sense of smell, revealing its significant susceptibility to cues from other senses. Contrary to common assumptions, the study suggests that smell is not merely primitive and reactive but rather exhibits a high degree of sophistication and proactivity. The research (Pierzchajlo et al., 2024), conducted at the University of Stockholm, found that the sense of smell was considerably more influenced by predictive cues compared with sight and hearing. In the study, even in tasks devoid of visual cues, both the olfactory and visual regions of the brain became active when the participants attempted to identify unfamiliar smells. This finding underscores the unique processing mechanism of the olfactory system, which appears to prioritize the detection of unexpected odours (Pierzchajlo et al., 2024). The activation of the visual brain in response to unexpected smells suggests a clever adaptation – perhaps to visually identify the source of the odour. This function serves as a form of warning, alerting us to odours that deviate from our expectations. Given humans' inherent difficulty in recognizing smells without contextual clues, this integrated sensory response highlights the brain's adaptive strategy to enhance olfactory perception.

The study was conducted with adults, so extrapolating to children's behaviours remains to be established. What we do know is that, unlike sight and our other senses, the human olfactory system is fully mature at birth. Indeed, smell is among the very first senses that a newborn baby encounters. It serves as a crucial survival tool, offering essential information to identify the mother and locate the source of nourishment she provides (Schaal, 1988). Schaal's early study, supported by clinical evidence, reveals the potential involvement of olfaction in various crucial developmental processes, including infant–mother bonding, facilitating the establishment of a strong emotional connection. Additionally, olfactory stimuli contribute to the infant's emotional regulation and stability, aiding in the maintenance of a balanced emotional state. So, if you want to calm a baby, don't think of just soothing sounds and rocking movements but soothing smells too. Moreover, olfactory experiences influence the child's social interactions and adaptive behaviours, shaping their responses and adjustments to their environment and relationships. These findings underscore the significance of olfactory perception in the earliest stages of a child's development.

More systematic documentation of children's olfactory abilities is essential, particularly over extended periods. To date, only a handful of longitudinal studies have been conducted in this area. Martinec Nováková and Havlíček (2020) conducted one such study, utilizing scores from the "Sniffin' Sticks" test (Hummel et al., 1997) to measure children's ability to discriminate smells based on standardized olfactory stimuli. Their findings revealed predominantly minor effects of gender and test practice on odour identification and discrimination, with girls exhibiting higher performance in these areas. The researchers suggest that there are some possible gender differences in how the sense of smell develops in children. They propose that observing olfactory development over longer periods, exceeding the typical two-year timeframe, is necessary to gain a comprehensive understanding of how children's olfactory abilities evolve over time.

As for the difference in olfactory performance by girls and boys, and influence of age, research with adults shows that it is a combination of factors, rather than one alone, that explains the variance. Namely, Gögele and colleagues (2024) conducted a large-scale study involving a population-based cohort of 6,944 participants (screened to ensure they had no acute nasal obstruction) and examined various biological, social, and medical parameters connected to smell. Their study revealed that age, sex, years of education, and smoking status collectively accounted for approximately 13 per cent of the total variance in the data. Additionally, the study identified several medical and lifestyle factors that negatively impacted odour identification scores. These included positive screenings for cognitive impairment and Parkinson's disease, a history of skull fracture, stage 2 hypertension, and alcohol abstinence. These findings indirectly debunk some popular myths around smell, such as for example that all girls have a more sophisticated sense of smell than do boys. Rather, the findings underscore the complex interplay between physiological and environmental factors in shaping olfactory function among individuals and the nature–nurture interplay in explaining differences in individuals' olfactory ability.

Brain research on smell

Olfaction and brain research hold significant interest for biological researchers, primarily because olfaction is one of the oldest sensory systems in organisms. This ancient sense plays a critical role in enabling organisms to locate food, identify potential mates, and avoid predators. By studying the intricate relationship between olfaction and the brain, neuroscientists gain valuable insights into the evolutionary origins and adaptive functions of this sensory system. In a study aimed at mapping the functional neuroanatomy of the olfactory cortex, the highest activation probability was revealed in the amygdala, piriform cortex, orbitofrontal cortex, as well as in the insula. Strong and reliable activations were observed in cortical structures previously identified as the primary and secondary olfactory cortices. These structures include the piriform cortex, which is a brain area that receives direct input from the olfactory bulb, and other brain areas receiving indirect input from the olfactory bulb, such as the amygdala, insula, and the orbitofrontal cortex (Torske et al., 2022).

Further to neuroscientific functional magnetic resonance imaging (fMRI) studies, research examining changes in the brain following olfactory training have indirectly shed light on the connections between neuroanatomy and the olfactory cortex. Namely, a systematic review revealed associations between olfactory training and increases in the volume or size of olfactory-related brain regions, notably the olfactory bulb and hippocampus, as well as alterations in functional connectivity (Vance et al., 2024). What is particularly intriguing is that these positive effects extend beyond patients with smell loss (hyposmia and anosmia) to include "normosmic" participants – those with a normal ability to smell. This suggests that olfactory training holds promise for enhancing olfactory function and potentially improving overall sensory processing, regardless of one's natural ability to smell.

The exact reasons for age-related olfactory impairment remain unclear. However, numerous brain studies have consistently shown that olfactory dysfunction frequently occurs early in neurodegenerative diseases (see Tremblay et al., 2022). This impairment is considered a potential marker indicating the progression from normal cognition to mild cognitive impairment and eventually dementia. For example, olfactory dysfunction has been associated with conditions such as Alzheimer's and Parkinson's disease (Rahayel et al., 2012) and it has also been noted in infectious diseases like COVID-19 across multiple countries (Mullol et al., 2020). By acknowledging these differences in olfactory perception between adults and children, and between individuals with normal or impaired ability to smell, we can better understand and support children's olfactory experiences.

To me, these findings instil a sense of urgency to foster the sense of smell from a young age.

Rather than waiting until olfactory ability diminishes, we can proactively engage with smell through early education and engage in more prevention than curation work. This applies to both educational research and practice. To illustrate with a specific project, the artist Peter de Cupere and his project "Smelloflowers" are a great example of how to stimulate a working sense of smell. "Smelloflowers" features a collection of stainless metal flowers embedded with fragrances placed in the centre of a nursing home hall. These flowers help stimulate residents' senses and provide orientation within the environment, with different departments matched to specific smells emitted from the flowers. Expanding on this concept, we can leverage artistic projects to stimulate children's sense of smell during their developmental stages and strategically embed it into architecture and learning resources. By integrating focused olfactory stimulation into childhood experiences, we not only enrich sensory development but also potentially safeguard against future health challenges linked to impaired olfactory function.

My suggestion links to the idea of "olfactory intelligence", which involves knowing about not just bad and good smells, but also the intensities and their presence in the air. Olfactory intelligent people will strategically introduce various odours around them to increase their concentration levels or help them feel relaxed. Marketing teams in restaurants, boutique hotels, and entertainment venues have known this for a long time. This knowledge could be brought to the design and support for olfactory engagement offered to children. Later in this book, I will describe an artistic project in which we created an exhibition where children could navigate the story events through their sense of smell. The impetus for the exhibition came from social sciences but it was also driven by the prevention agenda signalled by natural sciences.

Social studies and smell

Typically, social scientists and psychologists do not specialize in studying specific areas of the brain, but they frequently draw upon findings from brain research to explain phenomena such as the close link between smell and emotion. Smell stimulation directly happens in the emotional areas of the brain, which contrasts with the rational senses like hearing and vision that are processed in the cortex. As a result, olfaction and taste are closely associated with emotion-rich social processes such as mate attraction and religious practices.

In social sciences, the approach to olfaction is often discussed in terms of the opposing views between naturalizing senses and socializing them. For the latter, academic fields like the sociology of senses and ethnography delve into the moral, ethical, and political dimensions of sensory experiences (see Howes, 2021 for an overview). Unlike sight and hearing, which are often privileged in Western philosophical thought, taste and smell are considered "lower" senses in the hierarchy of senses (which some historians trace back to the philosophy of Immanuel Kant in the eighteenth century and some even further back in history to Aristotle in 380s BC). Historically, smell has been characterized as a purely chemical process that offers pleasure or displeasure without contributing significantly to higher cognitive functions such as thinking, language, or memory. However, social scientists have challenged this notion, suggesting that these senses play a crucial yet undervalued role in shaping social perceptions and behaviours. These researchers reject the hierarchical view of the senses proposed by Kantian rationalism and propose to focus on the social construction of the full spectrum of human senses, the sensorium (e.g. Howes, 2010; Merchant, 2011; Howes & Classen, 2013; Shiner, 2020).

As noted by Synnott (1991), odours play a defining role in shaping individual and group identities. Social scientists therefore examine the significance of smell in social interactions, particularly concerning class, ethnicity, and gender relations. This intersection between culture and senses highlights how smell contributes to the formation of social identities and the negotiation of power dynamics within society. As such, smell is viewed not just as a chemical sensation but as a symbolic expression. This approach challenges the fundamental equation that what smells good is perceived as good, and what smells bad is associated with negativity or evil. These simplified equations are not only symbolically used in children's fairy tales – they are real patterns studied by social scientists in intergroup relations where smell was used to legitimize power differentials.

In a historic review of smell use in social interactions, Classen (1992) outlined how, throughout history, smell has contributed to the exclusion of certain groups, perpetuated class systems, and fuelled discrimination. A close examination of these patterns reveals how cultures often categorize themselves as "us" and others as "others", with unpleasant smells serving as a powerful discriminatory factor. Additionally, Classen's analysis highlights how the perfume industry in Western culture has played a role in shaping perceptions of desirable smells: those who smell good are those who exhibit greater attractiveness and desirability, both for social but also commercial relationships (Classen, 1992). Furthermore, smell has been used by those in power to exclude and categorize others, leading to stereotypes based on odour, such as associating poverty with bad smells or certain ethnic foods with unpleasant odours. Recognizing and addressing these biases is essential for creating a more inclusive society.

The shift towards privileging sight and devaluing other senses like smell and touch can be traced back to the Enlightenment era, which emphasized empirical observations based on sight ("seeing is believing"). This bias led to an assumption of a visually dominated literature from which knowledge production was determined. But while the dominance of sight persists across academic disciplines, there has been a recent resurgence of interest in all the senses within the social sciences. This renewed attention is fuelled by a growing recognition of the importance of literacy as a multimodal practice, where literacy extends beyond static text to encompass a diverse range of modes.

Multimodal and multisensorial literacies

With an increasing presence in the field of literacy, critical literacy scholars are shifting away from traditional logocentric notions of reason, where the written word dominated. Instead, they are embracing sensorial experiences and their significance in understanding childhood and children's experiences, including those of reading and writing. These scholars view literacy as a lived multimodal and multimedia experience where different modes, such as words or images, sounds, gestures or movement, interact with different media, such as paper, computer or smartphones, to afford meaning. In the work of Rachel Heydon (e.g. Heydon & Rowsell, 2015; McKee & Heydon, 2015), both adults and children participate in literacy activities that encompass multiple modes through art, song, writing, and digital media. No single mode of expression is privileged; children have the freedom to express themselves through singing or writing, valuing both printed and embodied forms of meaning equally. Such a multimodal approach to literacy emphasizes a broader communication repertoire than that typically available to children in kindergartens or schools and highlights the unique entry point that an individual might have into literacy. For some children, dancing might be the preferred mode of expression while for others it is drawing or storytelling. Such a multimodal framework of understanding children's literacy is a great fit for integrating a multisensory focus and it inspired my own work, particularly through the writings of scholars such as Kathy Mills and David Howes.

Mills' (2015) study on diverse sensory literacies delves into a range of established and emerging frameworks within literacy research, skilfully incorporating a multisensory approach. In her pioneering work, traditional reading and writing models such as socio-cultural and multimodal literacies are juxtaposed with newer paradigms like socio-spatial and socio-material literacies. As one of the first scholars advocating for a multisensory approach to literacy, Mills introduced a fresh perspective to literacy studies, with research projects that incorporate innovative technologies such as 3D virtual interactions, that immediately engage multiple senses compared with conventional devices like tablets or desktop computers.

Along with other contemporary literacy scholars such as Jennifer Rowsell, Mills emphasizes the integration of senses in reading experiences, including the incorporation of smell alongside digital- and paper-based reading. Despite our innate visual orientation, favouring audiovisual media, Rowsell and other multimedia scholars acknowledge that this preference may not always fulfil our fundamental needs. While much of today's information is effectively communicated through visual or auditory channels, the importance we attribute to media consumption doesn't always align with our essential sensory needs. It follows that media that allow for the expression and engagement of multiple senses are not only a predictable but also a desirable evolution of multiliteracies (Kucirkova, 2024).

What I find particularly interesting is Mills' exploration of innovative technologies alongside new theoretical perspectives. As such, her work challenges the conventional notion of literacy as solely alphabetic, advocating instead for the concept of "multiliteracies". Multiliteracies were originally put forth by the New London Group (see Cope & Kalantzis, 2000) as a manifesto for recognizing linguistic diversity and multimodal forms of linguistic expressions and representation in the field, to expand pedagogy and theory in literacy. The group of New London scholars advocated for literacy teaching to move away from the rules of standard forms of the national language and monolinguistic approaches, instead recognizing differences in patterns of meaning from one context to another, which are the consequence of many factors such as culture, experience, and social domain. Multiliteracies also take a step towards recognizing that meaning is made in ways that are increasingly multimodal – in which written-linguistic modes of meaning interface with oral, visual, audio, gestural, tactile, and spatial patterns of meaning.

Through my research, I am adding to critical and multiliteracies theories the focused attention on the olfactory mode. Just like visual or tactile modes, olfaction can also help us make meaning. In one article, Ida Bruheim Jensen and I propose that olfaction is a legitimate way of communicating and should be part of multiliteracies (Kucirkova & Jensen, 2024). Critics may say that the focus on the non-linguistic aspects of literacy may contrast with the viewpoints of some cognitive- or neuropsychologists who adhere to a narrow definition of literacy and reading as being purely the cognitive act of decoding written letters. My initial work aligned with this narrow understanding, perhaps reflecting my own experience of the classroom environment and prevailing views on reading and writing. However, Mills highlights the transformative impact of the digital revolution on literacy, stressing the interactive nature of digital texts and the increasing importance of the involvement of all senses in learning. As such, the overarching message of Mills' work encourages educators to embrace technological evolution alongside the evolving landscape of literacy education. This message connects, albeit indirectly, also with the latest neuroscientific work on how individual senses complement each other. It also touches on the emerging field of "crossmodal correspondences".

Crossmodal correspondences

Professor Charles Spence, who currently heads the Crossmodal Research Laboratory at Oxford University, is a prominent figure in the field of crossmodal correspondences. I had the privilege of collaborating with Professor Spence on co-written articles, and he also served as an academic advisor for my project. His expertise has been invaluable in understanding how our senses interact with each other and with the environment, contributing to this emerging exploration of sensory perception. Crossmodal correspondences, or cross-sensory correspondences, play a crucial role in human information processing. Crossmodal correspondences can occur automatically, and have been shown to influence both late decision-making processes and, under specific conditions, perceptual integration.

An example of crossmodal correspondence is when individuals associate high-pitched sounds with small, bright objects positioned high up in space. Another example is correspondence between sounds and taste: when individuals associate sweet and sour tastes with higher-pitched sounds, and in contrast, when bitter tastes are associated with sounds of a lower pitch (Crisinel & Spence, 2009).

Understanding these distinctions can enhance educators' awareness of how sensory experiences can influence learning and classroom dynamics. According to Spence (2011), there at least three types of crossmodal correspondences: structural (e.g. loudness–brightness), statistical (e.g. pitch–elevation, pitch–size), and semantic (e.g. pitch–elevation, pitch–spatial frequency, loudness–size).

Crisinel and Spence (2012) conducted an experiment to determine how adults match pitch with odours and found that more complex odours were attributed to the pitch of string instruments, while pleasant and enjoyable odours were associated with the pitch of the piano. The researchers attribute these connections to crossmodal associations, which are independent of learned associations of odours with objects and are also different from the associations that people have between specific colours and smells. Just how exactly these different sound–colour–smell associations occur in adults is not clear and they are even less clear in children, who have a smaller vocabulary to describe what they perceive.

At the time of writing, there are virtually no learning resources for young children designed purposefully to accommodate crossmodal correspondences. And yet, the correspondences are crucial to understand if we are to design new technologies in alignment with the learning sciences. Merely adding more hotspots to touch on screen, or loud music to e-books, would not produce the learning stimulation that we could get if we were to take into account the natural ways in which the brain works. Similarly, adding smell to books without taking into account colours and textures would also undermine the learning potential.

You will see me frequently citing Professors Spence and Mills in this book, as these researchers produce field-defining studies that not only inform but directly shape the nascent area of olfactory education. In addition, David Howes' work on multisensory education and Classen's work on smell are particularly relevant for understanding the social and cultural dimensions of smell.

Socio-cultural dimensions of smell

The word to describe the study of smell's role in social relationships is "osmology", as proposed by Classen. Osmology concerns the various ways of smelling and sharing smells in cultures, as well as the close connection between space, time, and individual approaches to smell, which vary from person to person. These differences are often presented in literature as two distinct poles: the aesthetic dimension of smell, associated with feelings, emotions, and symbolism, as well as the artistic expression of smell; and the cognitive dimension, which is associated with cognitive functions such as thoughts, memories, and higher cognitive functions that extend beyond sensory perception. Howes skilfully navigates the tension between the aesthetic and cognitive potential of smell and aptly points out that in the Western tradition, smell has been a "temporal sense", connected to memory and recollection.

The cognitive approach to the temporal dimension is often elucidated through the Proustian moment, a widely cited example from the writer Marcel Proust. In this anecdote, Proust dipped a madeleine in his cup of tea and was transported back to his childhood, vividly recalling memories associated with the taste and aroma of the pastry. This experience, centred around the French madeleine cake, has been extensively studied by researchers in neuroscience. However, it is just one example of a larger phenomenon, with other literature offering similar experiences. Indeed, recent literature suggests that the complexity and ambiguity of Proust's text may have led to misinterpretations in scientific studies (Bray, 2013). Nevertheless, the enduring power of the madeleine as a potent olfactory memory cue remains, highlighting olfaction's role in triggering inward journeys into memory. It also highlights how much the research on olfaction is informed by the Western, or Global North, understanding of the world.

Howes (2024) reveals that in India and Sanscrit literature, or Japan and the incense ceremony, smell is positioned as a "spatial sense", which connects to outward stimuli (e.g. places to go). This is in contrast to the temporal Western understanding of smell as a sense that connects inward to one's memories. A holistic approach takes into account both dimensions.

My work resonates with a holistic inward–outward understanding of smell as a sense that allows for both temporal and spatial travels of the body and mind. It is that kind of spatial-temporal, cross-cultural understanding of smell that I hope to convey for early childhood educators. To concretize this idea in very simple terms, early childhood educators could initiate activities where children get on an olfactory hunt in the neighbourhood and document their perceptions in a smell map, and they also encourage activities where children close their eyes and focus on their sense of smell to remember specific events connected to a smell. Another example might be activities where bad smells are discussed and challenged with young children, nurturing their olfactory understanding where the bad smells are bad only in your mind.

In one study, we probed this connection between smell and culture further and directly asked parents of young children about what they think and do in relation to smell and the typical activity in Norwegian families: reading. In a national survey conducted with 1,001 parents of three- to six-year-olds in Norway, we investigated their reading habits at home in relation to the engagement of multiple senses (Kucirkova et al., 2023). In addition to asking traditional questions about how the parents read and whether they read to their children, we inquired about the importance of different sensory inputs during reading. These included the visual appearance of the books and lighting, any background noise while reading, the tactile quality of the books, and of course the surrounding smells, including the smell of the books themselves. Perhaps not surprisingly, smell was the least commented on by parents. However, when it was mentioned, it became evident that a positive and enjoyable smell was crucial for a pleasant reading experience. Similarly, noise was often discussed in terms of elimination if it was negative, loud, and disturbing. This highlights the similarity between smell and music I mentioned earlier but also how much parents influence what children get to experience during everyday routines (Kucirkova et al., 2023).

The parents' responses connect to Howes' thesis that senses (smell including) are created, perceived, and "lived differently" across the world and across different historic periods (Howes, 2024). Howes' work delves into various conceptions and perceptions of sensory experience and has been inspirational for me as I was trying to make sense of the role of olfaction in children's education. In his writings, Howes emphasizes that human perceptions are influenced by "technique", which offers a refreshing perspective on the active role we all play in training our senses. Specifically, how we train our sense of smell has implications for how we explore alternative ways of smelling and use smell strategically in various activities. Howes' approach marks a departure from the dominance of the "cognitive empire" and a shift towards a more holistic understanding of the body, where colours, senses, and lived experiences are viewed dynamically and relationally. Rather than "psychologizing" the senses, Howes advocates for "historizing" them, situating them within their historical and cultural contexts. It is in how Howes underscores the interconnectedness of the senses and their mutual modulation that I see most synergies with the crossmodal literature and multimedia work, such as that of Kathy Mills.

Furthermore, sensory learning aligns with contemporary approaches that highlight spatial and embodied educational methods, recognizing the complex entanglements of children's learning in diverse local and global contexts. Additionally, the focus on socio-spatial and embodied modes of learning underscores the significance of children's bodily responses and interactions within their environments. This line of work connects to what will be familiar to early education researchers and practitioners – the materiality and physical nature of early childhood experiences.

Smell and materiality

Readers might argue that the materiality of early childhood stands in contrast to the intangible nature of smells. Unlike physical objects that children can touch, smell is ephemeral and invisible, existing beyond the confines of space and time. Yet, despite its elusive nature, smell is undeniably real and *material*. Let me illustrate: through olfaction, there is a focus on the body because the brain only receives electrical impulses, while the body serves as a transducer, converting energy from one form to another. Thus, the brain itself does not directly experience sensations such as smell or sound; rather, it interprets signals received from the body. This distinction is particularly relevant in early childhood, where sensory experiences play a crucial role in cognitive and emotional development. During this developmental stage, children are actively engaged in exploring their environment through all their senses, including smell. As such, olfactory experiences not only contribute to a child's understanding of the world around them but also shape their emotional responses and social interactions. These are material.

While fairy tales often depict magical substances like "fairy dust" and "magic potions", the exact sensations they evoke remain vague and ambiguous. Indeed, olfactory perceptions seem often to develop outside of consciousness or our linguistic ability to capture the sensations. From this perspective, it is somewhat paradoxical that I am writing a book about olfaction using words, considering that olfaction is a particularly challenging domain to explore through language. Like other abstract concepts, such as time, odours can be difficult to conceptualize and to convey meaning from one person to another. An odour cannot be heard, seen, or held, making it challenging to locate in space, and most people struggle to articulate their olfactory experiences in words. However, despite these difficulties, there is a shared reaction when we encounter certain smells in a shared space – a material connection to our humanity. For example, a foul odour elicits a collective grimace, while the aroma of freshly baked bread evokes feelings of comfort. Imagine if we were to pay closer attention to these experiences as a means to better understand what unites us as human beings. This prospect holds great promise for inclusive early childhood education, fostering a deeper appreciation for the diverse sensory experiences that shape our shared human experience.

By considering these perspectives, multisensory learning carves out an emerging understanding of the role of olfaction in education. The intentional inclusion of olfactory training in educational curricula across various subject areas opens up possibilities for holistic education perspectives. As such, the "golden thread" weaving through the reviewed work in this chapter, for me, centres on the concept of smell as a sense that transcends traditional dichotomies in literacy and early education studies and opens up vistas for a more inclusive understanding of how learning happens.

Multisensory learning

Far too often, studies from individual disciplines tend to polarize between cognitive and emotional/aesthetic aspects of learning. The psychology approach often dominates developmental discussions, emphasizing measurable, data-driven insights as the only standard of establishing what works in children's learning. In contrast, other studies prioritize affective, play-based methods, where aesthetic and emotional dimensions take precedence. Another divide exists in literacy approaches, where reading is perceived either as traditional reading and writing skills, measured through standardized tests and focused on text decoding, or reading understood more broadly as meaning-making with various types of text. When applied to multisensory learning, these dichotomies reveal sensory learning viewed either as informing inward cognitive processes like memory or outward cultural perceptions shaping sensory meaning-making.

How can we bridge these dichotomies? Perhaps the attention to olfaction can act to cross the cognitive–emotional, aesthetic–academic, print–digital boundaries. The focus on olfaction prompts an understanding that emphasizes the fusion of multiple modes, senses, the body–mind connection. Thus, perhaps, olfaction can frame a holistic approach to literacy and early education.

2 The opportunities of olfaction in early education research and practice

If you're from a Western cultural background, chances are your education was heavily influenced by the belief that education primarily engages visual senses. This notion, championed by philosophers like Aristotle, and later echoed by Darwin, Freud, and Kant, has long elevated sight and hearing as the "superior" senses, while relegating others as "inferior". Consequently, concepts like olfaction-enhanced learning, or aroma-based learning, where scents are strategically integrated to impact learning, may be unfamiliar. Yet, the emerging field of olfactory learning explores the potential of various scents to enrich the learning process, whether by fostering concentration or enhancing the overall learning environment.

Olfaction can enhance educational experiences through two primary pathways: ambient smells in the atmosphere or integrated smells in either technologies or analogue learning resources. Ambient smells, dispersed throughout the learning environment via methods such as diffusers or natural ventilation, create an olfactory atmosphere. Alternatively, scent integration directly into learning resources can create olfactory resources. Olfactory resources can be created through techniques like scratch-and-sniff surfaces in books or emerging technologies that enable "smell teleportation", which seamlessly incorporate scent cues into digital learning platforms.

What potential educational applications does smell integration hold? For cognitive and psychology researchers invested in learning outcomes, the primary question is: can integrating smells influence learners' attention? The interest lies in, for example, the possibilities for learners to focus more on materials infused with specific scents, such as peppermint or orange. A strategic approach to investigating the cognitive connections involves comparing learners' attention to visual cues modulated by images, sounds, or olfaction.

DOI: 10.4324/9781003482024-2

Olfactory learning

A key learning mechanism is attention: if we pay attention, we are engaged and if we are engaged, we can learn. Could olfaction be part of stimulating attention? This is what intrigued Bodnar et al. (2004), who conducted an experiment exploring olfactory notifications. Rather than relying on visual or auditory cues, participants received bursts of scents to alert them to incoming messages, a concept with implications for future technology design. The study introduced olfactory modality as a potential alternative for delivering messaging notifications alongside visual and auditory modalities. Results indicated variations in the disruptiveness and effectiveness of notifications across modalities. While olfactory notifications were found to be less effective than other modalities, they were also less disruptive to user engagement in primary tasks.

In addition to attention, which is considered the key cognitive mechanism implicated in learning, the engagement of various emotions is key. In a study by Herz and Cupchik (1995), researchers explored whether odours triggered more emotional memories and discovered that both odour and verbal cues were equally effective in eliciting correct responses in adult learners, but that odours elicited more emotionally intense memories. The findings align with the anecdotal evidence regarding the connection between smells and intense childhood memories. Just how exactly to capitalize on these connections for learning is not clear. Olfaction could potentially be leveraged to direct attention towards crucial elements in the learning of factual information. This proposition has yet to be rigorously tested with child users given that olfactory learning studies primarily involve adults, and we currently lack similar research with children.

The learning properties of odours

Loewer (2006) conducted a review of various small-scale experiments with adults on learning and found that the key to higher learner performance is pleasant smells. Specifically, olfactory studies on learner performance show that pleasant aromas such as peppermint, rosemary, and lavender can be used to enhance concentration and learning outcomes. Various types of learning were enhanced in the experiments reviewed by Loewer, including students' performance on tests examining maths problems, vocabulary recall, and university students learning various types of content such as biology facts, for example.

Animal studies of olfaction provide some insights into the properties of specific types of smell, although extrapolating the effects to humans is very tricky. These studies typically involve rodents (mice or rats) and they examine the relationship between olfaction and various intrusive outcomes that would be unethical to study in humans, such as the introduction of anxiety, pain, or brain modulation. One such study particularly captured my attention: Ceccarelli et al.'s (2004) investigation into the prolonged olfactory stimulation of rodents using lemon essential oil. This study revealed significant effects on behavioural, hormonal, and neural parameters resulting from exposure to the oil, with some effects demonstrating sex-specific differences. Both male and female rats exhibited an increased pain threshold following extended exposure to the essential oil, suggesting the potential of olfactory stimulation to influence pain pathways and/or brain regions associated with pain modulation. Additionally, female rats displayed heightened reactivity to the stimulus.

Essential lemon oil is not only pleasant to smell (and often included in cleaning products) but is also known in aromatherapy for reducing inflammation, fatigue, and bacterial infections. In her Master's thesis at the University of Wisconsin, Nikora (2020) used lemon oil to investigate the effectiveness of olfactory stimuli through aromatherapy in a Montessori classroom. The study involved twenty-six children aged three to six years. Lemon essential oil was diffused using two diffusers placed in the classroom during the research sessions. Nikora assessed three aspects of the intervention's impact: the overall atmosphere in the kindergarten, noise level, and children's work engagement. The Overall Classroom Status Rating was evaluated at both the beginning (9.45 am) and end (10.30 am) of the experiment. Children's work engagement was measured by assessing engagement in five subcategories: using work as a prop, choosing work, receiving help, wandering/interfering, and behaving disruptively. Furthermore, ten children were interviewed about their feelings using an emoji scale to capture subjective reports of emotional status. It is important to note that these results are preliminary as the data were collected and interpreted by a single researcher without a full peer-review of the final published thesis. It is interesting to note, however, that Nikora observed that, contrary to her expectations of a calming effect, the lemon essential oil in fact stimulated the children. The exposure to lemon resulted in lower work engagement; that is to say, the children were mentally stimulated and more distracted for the tasks in the classroom. Nikora concluded that aromatherapy does have an effect and that careful choice of the specific essential oil is crucial.

This is a conclusion I agree with and, at this juncture of research, I emphasize the importance of carefully selecting specific scents for stimulating children's learning or emotions. For young children in particular, the safety of the oils used in interventions, their concentration levels, and their intensity are key to examine. For example, peppermint and citrus essential oils such as lemon are generally considered safe. However, there are important age considerations to take into account, with the youngest children (under three) not recommended to be exposed to essential oils. There are also important gender differences in how children respond to smell.

Gender differences in learning with smell

A widely reported finding in the literature is that boys and girls exhibit distinct responses to odours and demonstrate varying levels of awareness of different scents when assessed using standardized tests. Studies comparing diverse groups of children from different cultures, such as the study by Saxton et al. (2014) that compared the performance of children from Czechia and Namibia, have indicated that these differences are consistent across cultural groups. This implies that sex differences in olfactory awareness are apparent across a broad spectrum of cultures and age groups. Why is this so?

As is often the case with studies indicating varying effects among different groups of children, the diversity in outcomes could be attributed equally to inherent factors (nature) or environmental influences (nurture effects). One study, in particular, offers compelling evidence that children's awareness of odours is shaped by environmental factors, contributing to the gender differences observed in children's reactions to odours as highlighted in previous research.

Martinec Nováková and colleagues (2018) looked at how diversity in children's everyday exposure to various smells might influence their sense of smell and awareness of odours. The researchers tested 153 preschool children's olfactory abilities and odour awareness using questionnaires and the standardized SSParoT ("Sniffin' Sticks" Parosmia Test; Hummel et al., 1997). The test has been specifically designed to assess change to sense of smell. It comprises sticks with various odours, evenly divided into pleasant odours and unpleasant odours. The researchers not only tested the children but also surveyed parents about their children's exposure to different smells and their own awareness of odours. After controlling for children's age and verbal fluency, the study found that children's ability to identify and discriminate smells was influenced by their parents' odour awareness. Although the effects were small, they were similar in magnitude to those of gender and age. This study was the first to show that the variation in smells that children are exposed to at home significantly impacts their awareness of odours and actual sense of smell. In other words, the gender differences that are being observed in population studies are likely to be the result of boys' and girls' different exposure to smells. Indeed, Nováková et al.'s (2014) research revealed that a heightened exposure to scents among girls correlated with increased awareness of various odours. The stereotypical belief is that girls tend to engage more with perfumes than boys, and this has been linked to various side effects, but one possible positive side effect is that girls' increased exposure to perfumes trains their sense of smell. From this perspective, the exposure to diverse (natural and safe) scents should not be limited to girls or other specific groups of children but made available to all.

In addition to exposure to various odours, there are other factors at play, too. In another study, Nováková's team found that increased exposure to a wider range of possibly strong or new food scents and tastes, both during childhood and adulthood, was associated with enhanced odour awareness and improved odour identification (Nováková et al., 2014). This is a very important finding because we know from other studies that olfactory training is linked to improved overall cognition, particularly in areas such as verbal fluency and verbal learning/memory (Vance et al., 2024). This implies that the assumptions regarding exposing children to different odours are not merely speculative in relation to the potential positive impact on children's learning. Instead, this is evidently associated with children's enhanced ability to identify and be aware of a wider range of odours. This aspect can contribute to their language learning and even memory retention, regardless of gender.

Children have a keen sense of olfactory significance: they grasp and articulate the significance of scents from the age of five; smell matters to them not only for food but also for social relations. This is known from studies that compared children of various age groups and cultures (e.g. children from Scotland and Pakistan in the Sorokowski et al., 2023 study).

What I find particularly exciting when reflecting on these findings is how easy it is to integrate olfaction into classrooms. There's no need to invest in expensive equipment, technology, or costly field trips. Teachers can utilize the resources readily available to them in the classroom. This includes using everyday items such as food ingredients and natural scents found in the local environment, whether they come from plants, flowers, or herbs.

The cross-cultural research underscores why kindergartens and early childhood centres should provide equal opportunities for children to encounter various types of odours, both pleasant and unpleasant, and develop children's awareness of them. It is through the conscious identification of odours, discussing their origins and describing them with words, that odour awareness and related cognitive functions such as language and memory can be nurtured.

Nurturing children's sense of smell in kindergartens

For teachers or practitioners reading this chapter and interested in the importance of smell, the first question is likely how they can use it in their own settings. Researchers in this area might not have been quick to put ideas into action, leaving the practice of olfactory training with children in kindergartens mainly to artists and smell experts. One consideration is what to utilize: natural scents readily found in plants or foods are a good option. The intensity of these scents can be heightened by chopping and crushing the plants or applying heat to foods. Naturally, the amount used also influences the effect. Another option is to use essential oils, which are derived through mechanical pressing or distillation. These highly concentrated botanical extracts preserve the inherent aroma and taste of their botanical source.

Every essential oil has a distinctive blend of compounds, and the compounds influence the oil's various properties such as the scent but also its physiological effects. One needs to be careful with essential oils because some of them – namely lavender and tee tree oil – have been shown (in some small clinical case studies, see Karan, 2019) to be being linked to health issues when applied to skin or used as part of perfumes.

Essential oils delivered through diffusers are a good possibility for early childhood education but, as mentioned, caution should be exercised regarding the type of essential oil and its concentration levels. Sheppard-Hanger and Hanger (2015) proposed that essential oils can be administered to children aged two years and above in a similar manner as to adults, albeit with reduced quantities. Although there is no research showing direct harm, the current guidance recommends that essential oils should not be applied to babies and children under the age of two. The suggested dosage for children aged three years and older is approximately six drops in a 30 ml bottle, equating to a dilution of 1.5 per cent or lower. For children over six years old, a recommended dilution of 2.5 per cent or less is recommended.

Continuing on the note of practical applications of olfaction in education to increase children's exposure to diverse scents, I outline three projects that utilized research-based approaches to incorporate sensory learning with olfaction into early childhood education. These endeavours, led by researchers, demonstrate how researcher–practitioner collaborations can provide valuable insights into the potential outcomes when sensory awareness and olfaction are integrated into practice.

Research-practice projects in olfactory education

Professor Emilie Sitzia, based in the Netherlands, spearheads a project focused on senses-based learning: https://sensesbasedlearning.org/ Described as a "pedagogical methodology for tertiary education", the project emphasizes the exploration and enhancement of sensory skills, along with critical reflection on their significance in research and professional practice. The research group has also developed a learning manifesto advocating for increased awareness of sensory learning in education. The project website is a treasure trove of ideas in how greater attention to all senses, olfaction included, can enhance learning.

While the primary audience is adults, many of the techniques, including detailed instructions for lesson plans and teacher tools and techniques, can be adapted for use with children. Take, for example, a lesson plan inspired by Marres' Workshops "Training the Senses". This activity suggests combining art, smell, and synaesthesia to stimulate all the senses in two simple steps: first, children smell paper samples dipped into vials containing different scents. These vials are small glass containers commonly used for holding liquid materials such as odours and are often seen in aromatherapy. Teachers or practitioners can fill these vials with essential oils and then dab a drop onto paper for the children to smell. Next, the participants are asked to reflect on how the smell makes them feel. This activity can easily be adjusted for younger children by encouraging them to express their emotions using emoji faces displayed on cardboard, where they can mark how they feel. Alternatively, they can be invited to draw what the smell reminds them of.

This simple set-up can be easily adopted for any kindergarten. Teachers can use natural smells to stimulate discussions and emotional responses in children to various smells found in their surroundings (e.g. the smell of breakfast cereals or the paper smell of books). Expanding the olfactory stimulation to literacy, kindergarten teachers can integrate poems or fictional stories into smell activities. For example, the humorous poem, "My Senses All Are Backward" by Kenn Nesbitt is a great way to bring some humour into the session and encourage children to think about both positive and negative smells. In the poem, the main narrator experiences their senses all mixed up, with smells typically perceived as pleasant, like roses, described as terrible, and odours usually considered unpleasant, like skunks, depicted as enjoyable. Other senses, such as taste, are also invoked in the poem, with the narrator expressing a distaste for chocolate, which children may find amusing. This technique of reversing the perception of smells, as seen in the poem, can elicit laughter and spark conversations about how different smells are perceived as positive or negative.

The poem can be found on Kenn Nesbitt's Poetry4kids website (https://poetry4kids.com/), along with several other poems teachers can use for this aim. The creative practitioner might want to adapt this exercise for writing new rhymes for the children, incorporating smells the children say they dislike and describing them as pleasant, and vice versa. Such an exercise is a fantastic way to enhance odour awareness in young children, combining language and literacy with sensory learning and involving children in olfactory literacies.

On the topic of creativity, older children can explore their poetic talents by writing their own scented poems. The Fragrance Foundation's Marty the Mighty Nose Awards previously organized a smell-inspired poetry competition for children aged 7–11, with a specific focus on the sense of smell. Again, this could be a fantastic activity to adapt in local settings. Teachers could encourage children to write poems about smells they encounter on their way to school, for example, or perhaps new smells they have recently discovered and emotionally responded to. Is there a perfume they like, a plant that intrigues them, or a food that smells nice? What might be the types of chemical compounds in the different smells that the children like or dislike?

By stimulating these connections, children express themselves through poetry while also enhancing their appreciation for the sense of smell. Alternatively, to elicit children's responses to smells and incorporate them into literacy activities, you can integrate smell with storytelling. This is exactly what we did in our research study that we conducted in local kindergartens with an early years teacher.

In this study, we asked children to create stories that incorporated various scents, some imagined and some real, with the aim of encouraging them to consider the role of smell in narratives. This approach was implemented in collaboration with Monica Kamola in Norway (Kucirkova & Kamola, 2022), with the methodology known as "cultural probes". Cultural probes are commonly used in design research with children and involve providing participants with materials to explore and use in creating their own stories. The cultural probe we introduced was essentially a "story box" containing various open-ended materials such as wooden sticks, pompoms, feathers, wooden figurines, pencils, and drawing and painting supplies, enabling children to craft their own three-dimensional narratives.

This kind of technique had not been used in Norwegian kindergartens before; it is something that is often employed in design studies, allowing children to be involved in design projects and have their voices incorporated. Our aim was similar in this study, as we wanted to directly hear from children about the kinds of smells and scents they would mention in the stories they created, without the constraints of a specific literacy genre, expectations for publication, sharing, or producing the smell. The idea was to let children's imaginations run free. What we found was that children's imaginations are an amazing source of new smells that we had not considered incorporating into stories for them before. Some boys talked about the smell of spaceships and the universe, and some girls mentioned smells of animals or insects we thought didn't have a scent, such as butterflies. This study taught us the important lesson that allowing children's fantasy to run free can generate new experiences, something that should be more centrally present in discussions and practices when constructing new resources for children that involve olfaction.

The significance of open-endedness and the combination of creativity with olfaction are a central aspect of artistic projects, as seen in various works explored by olfactory artists. However, these endeavours have primarily focused on adult exhibitions and activities. One example is the artistic approach taken by Saskia Wilson-Brown, the founder and director of the Institute of Art and Olfaction. While many of these projects may not be suitable for children, one in particular caught my attention as it could be adapted for kindergarten practices.

In the Institute's activity "Sensing: ____" (https://artandolfaction.com/), participants link olfaction with existing artworks. The (adult) participants are encouraged to think and describe the connections between paintings and the senses of scent, taste, sound, touch, and sight. The multisensory commentary offers a unique way to engage with the artwork, a concept that galleries worldwide are exploring. Just imagine introducing this idea to kindergartens by exploring various artworks created by the children and discussing the scents they might represent. Alternatively, you could set up an art gallery of the children's artworks and infuse the room with a pleasant scent to enhance the overall experience.

The artwork project aligns with the theme of olfaction as a means to encourage children to communicate and explore literacy through various forms of expression – a concept that Kathy Mills would describe as multimodal sensory literacies. It shares similarities with art in its open-endedness, incorporation of multiple forms of expression, use of multimedia, and an unconstrained approach to creative expression.

Another inspiring project is that run by the Australian Catholic University, in Australia, called Sensory Orchestration (https://www.sensestogether.com). This project is led by Professor Mills' team and the focus is on multimodal literacy learning in primary education. This project stems from the understanding that everyday literacy practices are now both digital and multimodal, incorporating various modes such as written and spoken language, images, gestures, touch, movement, and sound. The theoretical framework of the project aligns with this premise. It uses innovative sensorial education programmes implemented in primary schools, digital labs, and art museums to develop a next-generation approach to multimodality. Over the years, the project has generated several journal articles, chapters, and books, providing clear guidance for incorporating digital multimedia and multisensory learning in primary and middle years.

The activities encompass tips tailored for older children and use of digital technologies, such as the activity "Sensory Brainstorming". In this activity, students are equipped with digital cameras, which can be those that are integrated into iPads or smartphones, allowing them to gather images, sounds, and videos associated with all five senses. Subsequently, children engage in discussions centred around these images, paying attention to how each sense is depicted and activated. This exercise serves not only to foster sensory awareness but also to enhance critical literacy skills.

As we explore ways to engage children with different smells and scents, we need to be aware that these scents can sometimes become overwhelming. One simple tip to cleanse the nostrils is to provide children with a small box of coffee beans to sniff, although this method has limited effectiveness. A more effective approach might be to limit the number of scents used in a session to a maximum of five for kindergarten children and to ensure there is good ventilation in the area and children take breaks.

That said, there are new technological advances aimed at addressing the issue of olfactory saturation, with many inventors in the perfumery industry leading the way. Major companies like Puig, which owns the famous fragrance brands such as Rabanne, Carolina Herrera, Charlotte Tilbury, Jean Paul Gaultier, Nina Ricci, and others, are developing and refining olfactory transmitters to allow for larger quantities of fragrances to be smelled in one session. One of the futuristic initiatives driven by Puig is Air Parfum, which aims to address the challenge of oversaturation of the sense of smell in shops and shopping malls. The Puig device allows customers to select and test perfumes using a tablet, emitting the scent with less alcohol and more air to prevent olfactory saturation. Individuals can create their own olfactory profiles, so that the device can select relevant fragrances based on these preferences. The application to children's olfactory activities is far away at this stage, but it might become possible as more projects incorporate smells into everyday activities.

Olfactory story exhibition

At one stage of our project in Norway, we explored the fusion of art, emotions, and learning experiences. Our goal was to develop materials that would capitalize on children's unique responses to smells and scents in their stories. Building on the participatory research approach we had at the start of the project with children making their own stories with smells, we aimed to expand on this concept by integrating it with learning experiences and the idea of multimodality, as embedded by the literacy and learning projects led by others. To achieve this, we partnered with a local children's museum and exhibition space in the Stavanger area (Vitenfabrikken) and adopted a community approach. We collaborated closely with Vitenfabrikken's staff, local librarians, an olfactory expert, several researchers, and a children's publisher, resulting in the creation of the children's first story-inspired olfactory exhibition.

The exhibition featured the classic fairy tale "The Three Little Pigs". We chose this traditional story because we assumed it would be familiar to most children and provide a narrative structure that we could enhance with smell, stimulating multiple senses. To complement the storytelling experience, we equipped the exhibition space with olfactory boxes, specially crafted by an olfactory artist, and audio materials recorded at the university. Additionally, we collaborated with the museum to create small wooden sheds where children could immerse themselves in the story scenes. These sheds were adorned with various artifacts, such as stove replicas and small flowers in the brick house, along with books and pillows for seating. Children were invited to the exhibition through their kindergartens, and some visiting children participated in our research project, which we reported on in a series of research articles. Following the research phase, the exhibition was open to the public.

It featured five olfactory stations, each representing a different point in the story. At the first station, visitors encountered the scent of the pigs' house – a pungent odour of urine and pigpen, indicating their living quarters. This smell emanated from a wooden box with a perforated surface, concealing cotton balls saturated with the smell. The box's lid was coloured in the colour corresponding with the type of smell, for example dark yellow was used to match the atmosphere of the unpleasant odour.

Moving on to the second station, visitors encountered the house of the Vain Pig, who, in our version of the story, preferred leisure over work, residing in a straw house vulnerable to the wolf's attacks. The interior of the house was adorned in various shades of pink, including the pillows and walls. A mirror hung on the wall, emphasizing the pig's vanity. The corresponding odour chosen for this station was a sweet and fruity fragrance reminiscent of lipstick or candy, complementing the pink colour scheme.

At the next station, visitors encountered the dwelling of the Reading Pig, characterized by his love for reading and his sturdy wooden abode. Inside the house, the ambiance exuded an air of tranquillity and erudition, with shelves filled with books and comfortable pillows inviting children to sit and engage with the books. The olfactory experience was carefully curated to emulate the scent of wood, enhancing the immersive journey. A green lid was integrated with the wooden box, harmonizing with the serene atmosphere and evoking a sense of natural outdoor environment. The presence of books further enriched the environment, fostering a sense of intellectual curiosity and inviting children to just sit, relax, and read.

Next, visitors arrived at the station dedicated to the Resourceful Pig, who constructed a sturdy brick house to thwart the wolf's advances. This station aimed to evoke feelings of warmth and security, resembling a cosy kitchen setting complete with a small table and a play stove. Positioned atop the stove was a pot containing the olfactory box, emitting a delightful aroma crafted to mimic the scent of chocolate. The box itself was painted brown, intended to match the colour of chocolate and enhancing the thematic cohesion. To further enhance the atmosphere of safety and comfort, the space was illuminated with soft, dimmed yellow lighting.

The most challenging odour to capture for the exhibition was that of the bad character in the story – the Big Bad Wolf. Rather than incorporating a visual representation of the menacing wolf, we opted to keep it unseen during the exhibition. We suspended an artificial paw with claws from an artificial pine tree, beneath which we placed the box containing the wolf's smell. This smell was intentionally designed to linger in the air, even when the box was closed, reminiscent of the bad smell of a wet dog. Its presence evoked a sense of unease and apprehension, as it suggested the unseen presence of something ominous. A subsequent analysis (Kucirkova, 2023) revealed that this aspect was the most unsettling for the children, who commented on their unease both during and after the exhibition. In fact, some of our youngest visitors, aged just three years old, were hesitant to enter the exhibition at all due to their fear of the invisible wolf lurking within.

The children's fear could have been exacerbated by the sounds emanating from the loudspeakers positioned on the ceiling of the exhibition. These loudspeakers remained active throughout the exhibition, emitting occasional whines and huffs intended to evoke the presence of the wolf. Additionally, the exhibition featured a voiceover narration of the story, accessible via QR codes displayed on posters at each station. The voiceover narration was not continuously playing; rather, it could be activated by scanning the QR code, allowing accompanying adults to choose whether to engage with the full story. This provided flexibility in how visitors experienced the narrative, with some teachers opting to play the story sequentially from station one, featuring the pigpen, to the final station depicting the chocolate and brick house. Conversely, other kindergarten visitors explored the exhibition without listening to the story, potentially missing certain stations but selecting their preferred areas with pleasant scents.

As we were not aiming for specific learning outcomes such as children's comprehension of the story, we deliberately avoided providing any official guidance or prescribed sequence for experiencing the exhibition. Instead, we emphasized open-endedness and multiple entry points into the narrative. This idea of "multiple entry points to a story" included different starting points in the story and engaged with various senses – visual, auditory, and olfactory.

The feedback on the exhibition was overwhelmingly positive, leading us to extend its duration by several months. The Vitenfabrikken staff and kindergarten teachers commented that the children particularly enjoyed the freedom to move around and fully immerse themselves in the space. Unlike traditional museums, where touching exhibits is discouraged, here they could explore with their entire bodies, enhancing their engagement with the story.

While organizing an exhibition may not be immediately straightforward for all practitioners, our concept of a scented adventure trail and fairy tale could be adapted for early childhood settings. For instance, teachers could select natural scents like those from pine branches, orange peel, or cinnamon bark and place them along a trail for children to explore and smell. These scents could be hidden in boxes for children to discover and discuss together in an assembly or group discussion led by the teacher. The children could share their impressions of the scents and perhaps reminisce about encountering them before by recalling memories of smelling them at home or in other places. This is likely to spark engaging discussions about connections to home and opportunities to expand the scent collection with favourite smells children may want to bring from home to kindergarten (a box could be a suitable format for this).

Another creative idea stemming from the project involves pairing smells with different story characters. In our exhibition, the elegant character was associated with a sweet smell and the colour pink, while the studious character had a green colour and a pine scent. We chose to link smells with colours because there is a recognized connection between the two sensory experiences. This association appears to be consistent across cultures; for instance, both British and French adults tend to link the same colours with specific smells, indicating that odour information can be effectively conveyed through colours (Jacquot et al., 2016). Furthermore, the relationship between colours and smells is commonly utilized in food products, as studies have demonstrated that colours can influence our perception of odours. For example, an orange-coloured drink may be perceived as orange-flavoured, even if its actual flavour is strawberry.

However, although we were cognizant of the colour-coded association, we underestimated its power for an unexpectedly significant by-effect in our study. Namely, when we designed the cosy area with a brown lid and perforated section for the smell of chocolate, we assumed it would match the colour of comforting cocoa. However, many children, perhaps due to their young age, associated the brown colour with unpleasant smells (such as poo), and were hesitant to open or smell the box. Even when they did smell it, despite the scent being clearly chocolate to adults, the children reported it smelled like "poo". This phenomenon, known as synaesthesia, occurs when one sense involuntarily triggers another, such as seeing brown causing children to perceive a bad smell, even though the actual scent is pleasant.

Synaesthesia's significant influence on perception is well documented in children's studies, particularly regarding food. This association can lead children, especially young ones, to refuse foods with dark colours, as food preferences are strongly intertwined with synaesthesia (Ward, 2013). Just how much these different associations are a result of the environment or of innate differences was highlighted in an observational study with adults and children, specifically focused on associations with odours and other (sound, touch) modalities. What Speed et al. (2021) found is that the associations are largely based on children's experiences rather than innate differences. Synaesthesia research thus further underscores that the more varied and diverse experiences with smell and other sensory modalities children have, the better for their perceptions and actual cognitive functioning.

In sum, the simple yet engaging activities outlined in this chapter not only stimulate the senses but also encourage children to express themselves creatively and develop their odour awareness. They show that smell can be part of everyday activities in the kindergarten and several open-ended activities. Another way of including smell into everyday activities is to connect it directly to existing routines, such as book reading. As detailed in the next chapter, olfactory reading, and embedding smell into children's books, is an exciting area of research practice in early childhood. It starts with developing our understanding of olfactory literacies – how smell works and why.

3 Developing olfactory literacies

The previous chapter encouraged us to consider how adults might facilitate sensory learning opportunities that foreground smell. This chapter aims to provide insights into the research approaches in olfaction and to offer suggestions for educational researchers on fostering olfactory inquiries. The idea is that, through a concentrated focus on olfaction, we can develop a fluid understanding of smell, and nurture both adults' and children's olfactory literacies.

I advocate for a participatory approach to olfactory research, ensuring it is not top-down from researchers to practitioners but rather a collaborative endeavour where innovation in practice informs innovation in research and vice versa. In emerging areas like children's learning with olfactory stimulation, a participatory approach that closely connects practice and research is preferable. This approach can safeguard against a nascent field that becomes dominated by technological innovations, which can often drive the agenda of new research. With significant interest in generative multisensory experiences driven by technological possibilities such as augmented reality (AR) and virtual reality (VR), it is crucial to prioritize the critical question of whether such experiences are genuinely desirable. By involving practitioners in the research process, we can ensure that the focus remains on the educational value and developmental benefits for children, rather than on the novelty of the technology itself.

Each research inquiry needs guiding questions and accompanying methodologies that align with these questions. To begin, we must start with the basic mechanics: how does smell work? When I first began studying smell, I was astonished to find that, even in 2024, despite our advancements in creating telescopic smell transportation across distances, we still lack a comprehensive understanding of how smell actually works. There are theories, but they are still being debated, and the science is far from settled.

DOI: 10.4324/9781003482024-3

We do know that almost all smells are made up of five key atoms: carbon, nitrogen, hydrogen, oxygen, and sulphur. But how do these elements work together for humans to recognize smells?

The mechanisms of smell

There are two key theories that have made some progress in explaining why things smell the way they do. One theory, proposed by Amoore in the 1950s (Amoore, 1952, 1963), is known as "Shape Theory". This theory posits that smell functions when receptors in the nose recognize the shape of molecules. However, even proponents of this theory admit that it doesn't explain all instances of olfactory perception.

The opposing theory is Luca Turin's "Vibrational Theory", which suggests that receptors in the nose recognize molecular vibrations, similar to how our eyes and ears perceive light and sound vibrations. Turin (1996) posits that the ear, eye, and nose are all vibrational senses. Essentially, your sense of smell could be much more like your sense of hearing, where your nose "listens" to the acoustic/vibrational bonds of aroma molecules. This theory potentially resolves many issues associated with Shape Theory.

Turin described how molecules have bonds connected to them that vibrate at specific frequencies, which are unique to each molecule and the bonds that connect them. Each unique smell corresponds to a unique vibration. To detect these molecular vibrations, Turin theorized that we must have a kind of spectroscope in our nose. However, this idea faced significant pushback from the scientific community immediately after Turin proposed it.

The controversial nature of scientists dismissing each other's theories is vividly described in the popular book *The Emperor of Scent* by Chandler Burr (2002). The book tells the story of how Turin struggled to gain recognition of his theory by biologists, even though he believed that Vibrational Theory, if validated, could revolutionize the perfume industry. That revolution hasn't happened yet and one notable piece of counter evidence comes from Block et al. (2015). Block and colleagues argue that there is no experimental data at the molecular level that would show direct evidence of electron transfer or the effect of odorant vibrations being responsible for triggering odorant receptor responses. This lack of molecular-level evidence challenges the validity of Turin's Vibrational Theory.

There have been several experimental works concerning Turin's proposed mechanism, but the jury is still out (Hoehn et al., 2018). Nevertheless, since proposing his theory in 1996, Turin has been creating synthetic aroma chemicals by calculating odours and their components rather than relying on traditional perfumers. He does this by calculating the vibrational spectrum of a molecule and using computer algorithms to find other molecules with related vibrations. Turin's approach is controversial and goes against what many perfumers believe perfume art should be about, which traditionally is an emphasis on creativity and intuition over purely scientific methods. Indeed, the art of perfumery is often described as communication through smells that elicits unique responses from each individual, which contrasts with Vibrational Theory that focuses on shared and universal vibrations and patterns, potentially overlooking the idiosyncratic nature of individual olfactory experiences.

These art-versus-science conflicts and research–industry controversies notwithstanding, it suffices to say that we still don't know how exactly smell works. Not surprisingly, when describing the workings of smell, researchers use various metaphors. The most popular is the music metaphor, as it aptly illustrates the complexity of olfaction while we await scientific consensus on its exact mechanisms.

Smell as a music metaphor

Like music, olfactory communication unfolds in real time, with a beginning and an end. Although the notes (or smells) are the same, people respond differently based on a combination of biological and cultural factors. Just as music has a basic "grammar" comprising notes, scales, and rhythms, olfaction also has fundamental principles. In music, notes can evoke a wide range of emotions and memories, and similarly, smells can trigger diverse responses. By exploring the connection between music and olfaction, we can begin to understand the basic "grammar" of smell, appreciating both the universal and unique aspects of our sensory experiences.

The nomenclature varies from language to language, but in English we distinguish in music grace notes, quarter notes, high notes, and low notes. In the olfaction and fragrance industry, we categorize them as top notes, middle notes, and base notes. In both music and fragrance, we speak of notes being in harmony, in accord. You can think of an accord as a typical combination of smells that go together, and these smells can then be divided into individual notes. A chord is an idea that consists of a blend of small ideas, like when you play a little tune or mesh several colours to create a new colour. This is how notes in odours combine too: just like in a chord there are three note types in a perfume: top notes, heart notes, and base notes.

The raw materials in fragrances have different lifespans when they come into contact with human skin. The smallest and most volatile molecules, which dissipate the quickest, are called top notes, and these are the notes that are smelled first. Top notes, also known as head notes, have a light molecular structure, so another way to describe them is through their size. Medium-sized molecules are listed as middle notes. The biggest notes that last several hours after application are the base notes.

When we mark the impression of a smell in workshops or our own practice, we write down the smell's "volatility". This refers to how quickly the fragrance disappears. Base notes have the lowest volatility; that is, the lowest ability to change rapidly and unpredictably. The quickest to disappear are the top notes, the accent notes, the most immediately perceived. These evaporate most quickly due to their light structure, within five to thirty minutes or so. Familiar top notes include lemon, berries, basil, and lavender.

Middle notes, also known as heart notes, are the notes that most people hold close to their heart and are part of most popular fragrances. They can be sweet and floral like rose, spicy like black pepper, or substantial like coffee. They last longer and linger more than the lighter top notes but evaporate within ten to sixty minutes.

Finally, base notes are the foundation: the woodsy, earthy scents that provide a lasting impression and give the heart notes something to connect to. These notes persist even when the top notes disappear. Base notes are the least volatile, evaporating more slowly than middle or top notes, and can last up to the whole day. They are therefore the most remembered. Examples of base notes include woods, vanilla, and patchouli.

There have been several attempts to guide the blending, the polyphony of odours and tastes, in a systematic way. In 1984, Ann Noble established the "Wine Aroma Wheel", defining a set of terms to describe the aromatic characteristics of wines, a model that has also been repurposed for other types of flavours and beverages. Similarly, Morten Meilgaard categorized beer aromas in the 1970s. In perfumery, the most widely known and used classification system is the "Fragrance Wheel", invented by scent expert Michael Edwards in 1992. This tool aids perfumers by placing families that share common olfactory characteristics next to one another. Families located closer together on the wheel are more likely to blend well in a perfume, whereas those further apart are less related. The four key fragrance families are amber, woody, floral, and fresh. Subfamilies adjacent on the wheel are most similar and thus likely to blend harmoniously. These families are based on specific notes.

What I learned in my Perfumery course was that the most common way to combine notes into common families is as follows:

Citrus: fresh and zesty notes from fruits like lemon, bergamot, and grapefruit.

Floral: flower notes from extracts like rose, jasmine, and lavender.

Oriental: warm and exotic notes of spices, vanilla, and amber.

Woody: earthy and grounded notes in scents like sandalwood, cedar, and patchouli.

Fresh/Aquatic: crisp and fresh notes like ocean or clean water.

The names of these families are easy to remember and can be one way of being more "literate" about olfaction when describing various everyday smells. Yet, although the focus on families or notes may give the impression that individual components make up individual smells, this would be an incorrect assumption. Take the example of rose. A rose is often used as a catchword to describe the rose smell but, in reality, it is a complex chemical composite. Rose extract consists of hundreds of compounds, contributing to its rich and multifaceted aroma. While commonly referred to simply as "rose", its precise chemical name is rose oxide, which is an organic compound that belongs to the pyran class of monoterpenes, with cis and trans isomers and each with stereoisomers.

These specifics in chemical composition are important, especially in the context of decomposing fragrances into their individual components for synthetic production. Namely, rose oxide can be industrially produced, addressing environmental concerns associated with harvesting real roses. This is particularly crucial for endangered species like the Bulgaria rose, which is highly sought after in perfumery but poses environmental risks if over-harvested. It is not only because of the environmental care that it is important to know the precise chemical composition of diverse odours; the precision in language can guide us towards precision in perceiving smells too.

Language and smells

The researcher-artist Sissel Tolaas, when interviewed as part of her project in Molecular Sampling of Volcanic Soil Carried out in Situ at the Archaeological Park of Pompeii, October 2022, was quoted as posting the pertinent question:

> Can the incorporation of my recorded smell molecules into existing archaeological knowledge contribute to the advancement of the field, as well as enabling the exploration of new dimensions of heritage (smell) and also potentially imbedding the smells into emotionally engaging artifacts and ecofacts?

While Tolaas' focus in her project was on adding the smells she has recorded to what we already know about ancient artifacts to help us learn more and potentially discover new aspects of history, this approach could also be applied to other areas of education, such as literacy, ethics, and olfactory language. To achieve this, we need to develop a nomenclature and clear language around the different smells we experience. For Sissel Tolaas, naming smells is crucial for establishing and preserving identities. When smells are named, they gain a tangible existence, can be remembered and utilized, and reflect the identities of their origins, whether human, plant, or animal. This concept is illustrated by Tolaas' work with the smells trapped in the walls of East Berlin and memories of war. By capturing and naming these odours, the artist heightened public awareness of the identities behind the smells, preserving the memories of those who witnessed past atrocities.

Academic researchers often emphasize the importance of naming odours due to the need for standardization, replication, and digitization. Naming and categorizing smells facilitate consistent communication and comparison across studies, enabling researchers to accurately replicate experiments and validate findings. Standardized odour nomenclature also supports the digitization of olfactory data, which is essential for advancing technologies that can record, reproduce, and analyse scents. This systematic approach not only enhances the scientific understanding of olfaction but also enables the integration of olfactory information into various digital applications. For instance, scent teleportation – sending smells from one location to another – is being pioneered by companies like Osmo, which has the tagline "giving computers a sense of smell" (https://www.osmo.ai).

Further advances in smell language were made by researchers at the Weizmann Institute of Science. Ravia and colleagues (2020) developed a framework for odours as part of a European initiative for Future Emerging Technologies, through an interdisciplinary project with neurobiologists, computer scientists, and a master perfumer. The researchers have made significant strides in demystifying even the most complex blends of odorants into their precise components to arrive at some common language. The framework enables computers to decode and replicate odours by converting odour perceptions into numerical data. This holds promise for digitizing and reproducing smells on demand.

As such, the historically closed world of perfumery becomes more open without diminishing the significance of the perfumery profession. Rather than disclosing the precise ingredients of perfumes, the olfactory language scientists therefore propose to record and map how various odorants are perceived. In that way, the study provides a unique example of how advancements in nomenclature bring clarity to what was once shrouded in mystery. Indeed, fragrances have for centuries been veiled in secrecy, understood only by master perfumers who have their own names for fragrances only they can detect. However, with the shift towards open science and community engagement in research, this exclusivity is gradually eroding.

Perfumes are crafted using a diverse range of ingredients and processes, encompassing both natural essences and synthetic chemicals. This means that perfumers must possess a deep understanding of these components to derive specific fragrances and chemically reproduce natural smells. As they immerse themselves in this task, many professionals no longer perceive scents in the same simplistic manner as a layperson might, who may simply describe the smell of grass as "smelling like grass". Instead, they identify individual molecules and compounds that contribute to the overall aroma. The olfactory experts are likely to say that it is the green leaf volatiles that increase their presence by cutting and think of the mixture of aldehydes and alcohols in the six carbon atoms that make up the unique cut grass smell.

The reason I am juxtaposing the perfumers' and scientists' approach to olfactory language is because it raises the question of how to approach olfactory education for future generations: should we train children to become more like chemists in olfaction or artist perfumers? While it may seem like a strange question, it is one that requires consideration, especially when developing educational materials.

Olfactory vocabulary

Words can sometimes hinder our ability to perceive and appreciate a smell, especially since our vocabulary for naming different odours in English is often lacking, unless we resort to describing the chemical components of the individual smells.

When exposing children to a strip with rose scent, the decision of what to teach them – whether to associate the smell with the concept of rose or with its chemical components – is pivotal. Each approach offers distinct educational benefits. Associating the smell with the concept of rose provides a cultural and contextual understanding of fragrance, connecting it to the world around them. Associating it with emotion delves into the subjective experience of scent, fostering emotional intelligence and sensory awareness. Exploring its chemical components introduces scientific concepts, encouraging critical thinking and analytical skills.

The most "educational" approach to olfactory education may vary depending on how one defines education. For some, it may prioritize scientific literacy and analytical thinking, favouring an emphasis on chemical components. For others, it may prioritize creativity, cultural understanding, and emotional intelligence, favouring an artistic approach. Naming the molecules may provide precise scientific knowledge, but it risks stripping away the artistic and unique associations that enhance our olfactory experiences. In formal education, where there is often a push for factual accuracy and precise naming of facts, these nuanced experiences may not always be welcomed. Ultimately, striking a balance between these approaches may offer the most comprehensive olfactory education. By integrating elements of chemistry, artistry, and language, we can empower children to appreciate the complexity of scent from multiple perspectives, fostering a deeper connection to the world of fragrance.

The more I engage with perfumers and olfactory artists, the more I realize how limited our olfactory language is among the general population compared with inside their circles. They effortlessly discuss the flowery scent of ylang-ylang or the woody notes of vetiver instead of resorting to lengthy explanations because there's a shared understanding of what each smell word represents. This is how language evolves – just like how you can train your ear to recognize various music tones and identify them in a song, you can do the same with odours. If we invent new words for smells, they might align with the crossmodal correspondences theory (Spence, 2011), where sharper and higher-pitched words would correspond to top notes like citrus and freshness, while deeper tones might evoke scents like vanilla. Would this work for children's vocabularies?

Studies have shown that children notice smells in things adults might overlook. For example, in one study, children described exploring a wonder world by saying, "Wonder world smells like cooking food and lavender" (Itenge et al., 2022). One thing I want to pass on to future studies is the need for balance as we consider various methodologies for researching and investigating children's sense of smell. Children have their own unique ways of expressing and understanding smells, and how they name these abstract, fantasy experiences is linked to their overall perception of smell. It is important to allow them to openly comment without diminishing their experience and the fantasy open-endedness with words that conjure specific images.

With an emphasis on centring the child's perspective, I now move to consider how olfaction can be studied using various research techniques.

Methods for measuring smell

As I have delved into researching different smell names, I have sometimes felt that I am "building the plane while flying it". I have found myself exploring various methodologies for studying smell with children while also measuring actual effects. Measuring olfaction holistically, rather than reducing it to only one method or qualitative versus quantitative approach, is crucial in such an emerging field. This is something that was advocated by the legendary olfactory researcher Trygg Engen. Engen, originally from Norway, was an eminent authority in sensory perception, particularly odour perception. He was a pioneering figure in the psychological study of olfaction, focusing on how to measure smell. In his books, *The Perception of Odors* and *Odor Sensation and Memory*, Trygg defined the field, and his work continues to impact contemporary olfactory scientists. Among these are Rachel Herz and Benoist Schaal, two of my olfactory research heroes who closely collaborated with Engen and furthered the study of olfaction.

Trygg's work included psychophysical measurement of olfactory sensation, olfactory perceptual development, and the roles of language, context, and expectation in odour experience, as well as environmental air and smell perception. It was the combination of findings from multiple sources that allowed him to arrive at new discoveries. Engen carried out numerous experiments to determine how people identify and label various smells with different kinds, intensities, and numbers of smells and he also delved into understanding how many smells one can handle without confusion, whether these should be presented in sequence or randomly, and the challenges of remembering and recognizing odours. These issues remain central to olfactory research today.

Notably, the way odours should be classified, and which names should be used to describe different perceptions of odours, continues to be debated. Despite these challenges, it is possible to determine the olfactory ability of an individual in a reliable and standardized way.

The "Sniffin' Sticks" test (Burghardt®, Wedel, Germany) is a standardized measure of olfactory abilities, developed by Hummel and colleagues in 1997. These tests have been calibrated with high reliability across multiple studies and are suitable for both adults and children. The test is unique in that it combines odour identification, discrimination, and threshold measurement to provide a thorough understanding of an individual's sense of smell. To illustrate how the test works you can imagine felt-tip pens filled with odorants. When the cap is removed, the odour is released. The pen is held approximately 2 cm in front of the nostrils, and the patient is asked to sniff when instructed by the tester (usually a clinician or a researcher). During the test, the patient is blindfolded with a sleeping mask and, in some cases, they have one of their nostrils blocked to test the nostrils separately. The test comprises three parts:

1. A Threshold test that determines the point at which the participant can correctly identify the butanol or phenylethyl alcohol (PEA) odour twice in a row at the same dilution. This dilution serves as the starting point for threshold measurements.
2. Discrimination of Odorants tests, whether participants can distinguish between different odours whereby the patients are given sixteen sets of three pens each. Two pens in each set contain the same odour, while the third, with a green cap, contains a different odour.
3. Identification of Odorants where the participants are asked to identify the odour from one of four options provided. This "forced choice" must be made even if the participant is uncertain or believes they did not smell anything. Rather than just asking whether the smell is good or bad, the participants need to select one of four options. For example, given the options "onion, sauerkraut, garlic, carrot", the correct answer might be only "garlic".

Gellrich et al. (2017) found that offering young children a maximum of three forced-choice answers works best. Further adaptations are being made to tailor the test for different types of users, but it remains the only well-calibrated and comprehensive approach for a detailed analysis of olfactory function.

Standardized approaches are excellent for establishing a clinical and consistent way to assess a child's sense of smell. These are different from more open-ended methods that focus on the child's experience and unique articulation of smells. The latter methods align more closely with the artistic tradition in olfaction, where experience and innovation are valued over rational cognition and standardization.

Artistic olfactory methods

How do we capture the ephemeral nature of smell as children move through different spaces? This question was pondered by multimodal researcher Kate Cowan, who explored how movement and spatial use contribute to the multimodal meaning-making process in children's play. Her mapping techniques documented the fleeting dynamics of children's playful movements, incorporating sketches, photographs, and video stills that captured their activities in various environments. Our research team similarly endeavoured to create smell logs and smell maps, systematically documenting different types of smells, their intensities, origins (whether initiated by individuals or naturally present), and approximate durations within the space.

SmellLogs are not limited to adults or researchers; anyone can utilize this simple methodology to document the types and locations of various smells. A smell log is simply a log of different smells captured at regular time intervals, with attention to the type of smell, possible origin, and intensity. In our research projects, we often include also whether the smell was initiated by the adult or the child.

SmellWalks, often used with adults to explore urban areas and note concentrated odours, involve participants smelling trees, pavement, and objects they wouldn't normally bring close to their noses. Described as part of a "sensuous methodology", these methods focus on individual sensory experiences rather than establishing who smells better or identifying universally shared smells. Smell walks can vary in group size, participant versus researcher-led techniques, and the reinvention of the smell-walking process. While some researchers find this variation exciting and enriching, others call for standardization and the development of "protocols for multisensory sensewalks" (see Parker et al., 2024).

Connected to smell walks are smell maps, which are often created for urban areas using the noses of thousands of volunteers. In SmellMaps, children are encouraged to draw a map of the smells they encounter during neighbourhood walks, integrating this into their daily outdoor routines. This is part of smell visualization, an attempt to capture smell intensity in a given location (McLean & Perkins, 2020). In McLean's research, participants are encouraged to smell trees, pavements, objects, and anything around them that they would not normally bring closer to their nose. They reflect on how the smells of the city evoke the multiple co-existences we experience as humans in shared spaces. These smells bring us to different places and memories while being part of the same city.

While in Western culture, smell maps and smell walks are part of urban studies, environmental preoccupation, and artistic projects, other cultures have unique olfactory traditions. For example, in Japan, the interest in olfaction is deeply ingrained in various cultural rituals, such as the Kōdō ceremony, which is literally "the art of listening to perfumes". This ancient practice emphasizes a deep, meditative engagement with scents, fostering a refined appreciation for the subtleties of different aromas. Another example is the Japanese Awaji Island, renowned for its "koh-shi", or "masters of perfume", who craft the country's most sought-after incense sticks and Japanese incense. These artisans have honed their skills over generations, blending natural ingredients with meticulous care to produce complex, layered scents. The incense created by the koh-shi is used in various traditional Japanese ceremonies and everyday life, reflecting the cultural significance of olfaction in Japan.

Japanese olfactory practices such as Kōdō and the art of crafting incense highlight that a standardized technique of smell logs or smell maps cannot be simply taken to any kind of environment at any time. Olfactory experiences are intricately woven into cultural rituals, mindfulness practices, and the pursuit of sensory harmony in many Asian cultures. While these traditions are not in direct contrast to my work involving children in smell walks, they certainly offer a different perspective. During my engagements with children in smell walks in England or the United States, countries with high-stakes standardised curricula, teachers often enquired about the learning objectives, the added value of such experiences, and how to justify the time spent on olfaction in a busy curriculum.

That said, I have been fortunate to collaborate with some wonderfully creative teachers who were willing to explore together with me new approaches to children's engagement with smell and spend time on developing children's understanding of smell. In one study conducted in local kindergartens, we encouraged the children to draw maps of their neighbourhood walks. The children's drawings depicted a fascinating array of sensory experiences, including familiar scents and objects like strawberries and trees. However, there were also intriguing mentions of less conventional smells, such as the "Christmas tree" aroma (despite the walk occurring in spring), the scent of woodlice, or the fragrance of sand. It was evident that the children attributed smells to various natural phenomena that often go under the "olfactory radar" of us, adults. While the scents of sands or woodlice may seem unusual to adults, they nonetheless evoked vivid sensory memories for the children.

Language, as mentioned, plays a pivotal role in shaping our perception of odours, yet this perception is intricately intertwined with inputs from other senses. For instance, during eating, smell enhances the flavour and nuances of taste. This in turn influences smell perceptions. Such insights are significant in methodological considerations. For example, in observing children reading books in kindergartens amidst natural smells, we encountered challenges such as lingering kitchen odours influencing children's behaviour. This is not surprising when considering how even small droplets of smell can alter the taste of water. Even if the water has the same taste, a whiff of smell can deliver a different message to your brain about its taste.

This concept is utilized commercially in air up®, an invention from the Netherlands, which employs retronasal smell ("tasting with the nose"). The technology operates under the premise that what we smell is what we taste. The device uses capsules with scents that are released when users drink water from bottles. Instead of flavouring the water, as most manufacturers do, they enhance the taste with the surrounding smell.

I am learning about how olfaction works often through these commercial innovations, but perhaps no other researcher has been more creative and directly contributed to prototypes and actual products that translate complex olfaction-related ideas into practice than David Edwards. David Edwards is a Lecturer at Harvard University in the School of Engineering and Applied Sciences. He is the brainchild behind Obooks, the first digital olfactory books. Obooks are digital books with attached cartridges below an iPad to release smell when the child presses a hotspot in the digital book. Another of his inventions is a "food inhaler" that dispenses breathable chocolate. Edwards is also behind the Nimbus design, which resembles a salt shaker, and when activated, it releases a cloud of flavour over cocktails and delivers sensory experiences.

As commercial applications continue to evolve in shaping adults' olfactory experiences, I am hopeful that close collaborations between academia and industry will similarly propel advancements in olfactory research aimed at enhancing children's lives.

Olfactory learnings

Numerous studies have shown that children's responses to odours are learned, highlighting the unique nature of olfactory perception. Unlike our understanding of other stimuli, we lack a structured language for describing smells, making emotional associations particularly powerful. Unfamiliar odours are often met with immediate aversion in children, underscoring the critical role of learning in odour perception. Rachel Herz, drawing from decades of olfactory research, emphasizes the distinctiveness of olfaction compared with other senses. She notes that the initial encounter with a smell strongly influences future hedonic perceptions, illustrating the profound impact of learned responses to smells (Herz, 2009).

Herz's insights, as detailed in her book *The Scent of Desire*, underscore the remarkable development of our olfactory system. Unlike other senses, our sense of smell is fully functional as early as twelve weeks into foetal development, making it the first sense to mature. This early development allows us to begin learning about odours even before birth, as the amniotic fluid surrounding the developing foetus carries a variety of scents. What a mother consumes during pregnancy can profoundly influence her baby's flavour preferences. Indeed, studies have shown that maternal consumption of flavours such as garlic or anise during pregnancy can lead to significantly greater acceptance of these flavours by children later in life. Infants whose mothers consumed these flavours during pregnancy exhibited increased appetitive behaviours, such as turning their heads toward the odour, increased mouthing or sucking, and facial expressions indicating liking when exposed to the same odour after birth. Additionally, there was evidence of heightened arousal, as reflected in increased body movements, among infants exposed to these flavours prenatally compared with those whose mothers did not ingest or ingested less of the respective flavour during pregnancy (Hepper, 1995; Faas et al., 2000). These findings underscore the profound impact of maternal diet on early flavour preferences but also the power of early olfactory learning.

To me, this research also underscores the significance of approaching olfactory experiences with children thoughtfully and intentionally. It is crucial to consider the smells we introduce, as well as the timing and context in which they're presented to children. The intentionality behind curating olfactory experiences is key. A smell walk, with children drawing their smell map afterwards, can be great fun, but it should not be introduced for the sake of it: there needs to be an intention, an awareness, of its importance for a particular group of children there and then.

Whether it is creating environments that evoke positive memories through familiar scents, incorporating aromatic elements into educational activities to stimulate learning, or promoting mindfulness and emotional well-being through scent-based practices, being intentional about smell can cultivate a more sensory-aware and enriched approach for both adults and children. As Rachel Herz, (2009, p. 238) put it:

> I think that simple awareness of how amazing, wonderful, and incredible our sense of smell is, and how much pleasure, dimensionality, intensity, and meaning, it can bring to our lives, is the most essential olfactory knowledge that we need to enrich our lives now and in the future.

Olfactory learning in the future

Further avenues to enrich our sense of smell are inevitably linked to technological advances, raising a critical question: to what extent should we digitize olfaction without fully understanding its mechanisms and the diverse odours in our immediate environment? There is a concern that rushing towards digitization, driven by technological possibilities, might overshadow what is truly necessary for natural olfactory development.

We risk that in our eagerness to embrace new technology, we may neglect the rich, nuanced experiences of natural odours and their roles in our daily lives. In addition, there is concern in some quarters that by digitizing smell, we are essentially digitizing emotions. The nose has direct access to the amygdala, as elucidated in Chapter 1, thereby establishing a close connection to the intensity of the emotions we experience. Consequently, olfaction can be considered an "emotional sense", which carries significant implications if we are digitizing olfaction experiences for children.

Regardless of which side of the olfactory future optimism or pessimism you sit, it is crucial to balance technological advancements with a deep understanding and appreciation of the natural olfactory world, ensuring that we do not lose touch with the essence of what smell means to human experience. It is also crucial to preserve the many smells that define our environments and are at risk of disappearing due to biological degradation. Efforts to preserve the scents of endangered species are exemplified by various olfactory projects, such as "Resurrecting the Sublime" (see https://www.resurrectingthesublime.com). This collaborative project brought together cutting-edge scientific research and immersive installations, led by Alexandra Daisy Ginsberg, Sissel Tolaas, and a team of synthetic biologists at Ginkgo Bioworks, headed by Christina Agapakis, with support from IFF Inc. The project was specifically dedicated to the smells of extinct flowers lost due to colonial activity. Using tiny amounts of DNA extracted from the specimens of three flowers stored at Harvard University's Herbaria, the team employed synthetic biology to predict and resynthesize gene sequences that might encode fragrance-producing enzymes. Sissel Tolaas then reconstructed the flowers' smells in her lab, utilizing identical or comparative smell molecules. The process not only preserved the olfactory heritage of these extinct species but also created an immersive experience for visitors to engage with these lost scents.

Another innovative and field-defining project was Odeuropa, which applied state-of-the-art artificial intelligence (AI) techniques to cultural heritage text and image datasets spanning four centuries of European history. This project identified and traced how "smell" was expressed in different languages, the places it was associated with, the kinds of events and practices it characterized, and the emotions it was linked to. This multimodal information was curated according to semantic web standards, stored in the "European Olfactory Knowledge Graph" (EOKG), and then used to create new "storylines" informed by cultural history research. The storyline resources were prepared in different formats for different audiences, including an online "Encyclopaedia of European Smell Heritage".

These various examples of olfactory inquiry highlight that smell is a key aspect for innovating approaches to understanding the environment, our history, and, ultimately, ourselves as a human species. It follows that, in education, we need to pay particular attention to how smell is introduced and nurtured as it carries implications for not only current experiences of what and how we smell but also the future of these experiences.

Education represents a dynamic research domain, embracing quantitative studies centred on interventions, qualitative inquiries exploring phenomena, and mixed methods that blend the strengths of both approaches. Olfactory investigations should intersect with these diverse methodologies. In my own research, I have used an experimental within-subject design trial, systematically examining how children associate odours with reading, and I have also undertaken qualitative, open-ended exploratory studies, wherein children construct their own olfactory worlds through approaches like smell walk documentation. Each approach has yielded unique insights into this captivating subject area, and it is perfectly possible to combine them in one line of inquiry.

Ending the chapter, I'm drawn to acknowledge the fascinating duality between artistic, open-ended and idiosyncratic approaches versus research-driven, standardized approaches to understanding smell. A pivotal moment for me was visiting Sissel Tolaas' exhibition in Oslo in 2022, titled "RE______", leaving room for interpretations like "rethink", "reality", "remember", or "reveal". The exhibition masterfully balanced intentionality with ambiguity, allowing for individualized experiences while exploring the universal versatility of the "RE" prefix. Each exhibit captured the dual nature of smell: from stones infused with odours to the potent aroma of "money", which carried a profound political message. Given smell's symbolic, cultural, learned, and biological dimensions, I posit that a diverse array of methods at the intersection of art and science will be essential in fully unlocking its potential.

4 Olfaction and children's literacies

Smell is a beloved theme in many novels. Perhaps you too, like me, may have developed a fascination with scents and perfumery by reading classic works like Patrick Süskind's *Perfume: The Story of a Murderer* or *The Alchemist* by Paulo Coelho, or perhaps *Diary of a Nose* by Jean-Claude Ellena. These fictional tales vividly outline the obsessive passion one can develop when pursuing perfumery or the art of olfaction. All three novels provide a rich arena for exploring the human fascination with smell and deepening our understanding of its allure. Books, more generally, provide a wonderful arena for exploring and deepening our understanding of various fascinating smells and scents.

Perhaps no other activity is considered more educational and enriching for young children than reading. Children become readers by learning letters and the meanings of words. Reading is not an innate activity but one that needs to be nurtured and cultivated from a young age. While book reading is widely researched, especially in early childhood, my work on olfactory reading and the importance of smell in reading with young children was the first research project focused specifically on this topic. What have we learned so far? In this chapter, I will describe our findings and make connections to established reading studies that explore the sensory aspects of reading, emphasizing the importance of the body and the interaction of all modalities in the reading process. I will connect to critical literacy scholars (e.g. Burnett et al., 2014a; Sefton-Green et al., 2016; Comber, 2015; Lenters, 2016) and the broader framework of the sensory turn in literacy studies (Mills et al., 2022; Pool et al., 2023). By doing so, I propose further directions for this research, as we have just started to examine what could be achieved through the combination of smell and literacy.

DOI: 10.4324/9781003482024-4

Smell in books

Smell can be incorporated into reading in various ways. First, there are ambient smells that surround the reader in their environment, whether in a room or in nature where reading takes place. This includes the natural aroma of old libraries often mentioned by readers. Additionally, smells can be specifically introduced into books, such as in scratch-and-sniff books for analogue texts or oBooks for digital books. Smell integrations into books typically represent the smells experienced through words in the text.

However, there is also an implied smell in reading, conjured up in readers' minds through descriptive language and scenarios where smell is present. This imaginative aspect of olfaction allows readers to mentally evoke scents based on textual cues, enriching their sensory experience of the narrative. Both the tangible and imagined smells play significant roles in how readers engage with and interpret texts, highlighting the multifaceted nature of olfactory incorporation in reading.

Let me start by probing the connection between implied smell and the content of some popular children's books. My research team conducted a systematic review of the most popular children's books that reference smell (Kucirkova & Tosun, 2023; Spence et al., 2024). Drawing from a comprehensive search of children's picture books in both paper-based and digital formats, we identified three principal ways in which olfaction is currently embedded in children's literature. First, smells are often used to enhance the depiction of various objects, such as foods and plants, and locations within the story, intended to create a more vivid and immersive setting for the readers. Second, smell is frequently employed to add a humorous element to the narrative; for instance, the portrayal of strong or unusual smells can lead to funny situations that engage young readers and elicit laughter. Third, smell serves as a mechanism to encourage children's active participation in the story. By referencing scents, authors invite young readers to use their imagination and personal experiences with different smells, making the reading experience more interactive and engaging. Through these methods, olfaction acts as a multifaceted tool in children's picture books, enhancing the storytelling experience by making it more immersive, humorous, and interactive.

Our content analysis of 102 olfaction-related picture books resulted in five main categories of olfactory references: flower-related, food-related, bad smells, those associated with potty training, and those linked to other senses (Kucirkova & Tosun, 2023). We found that the use of smells in these books is relatively limited compared with the potential that a more nuanced integration of smells could achieve. Based on literary theories, we propose several recommendations for future books, which may interest anyone writing or selecting children's books.

First, smell could be used to increase the reader's immersion in the story, allowing them to become more absorbed in the plot by experiencing abstract smells that open up fantastical worlds. Second, olfactory references could usefully advance narrative arcs and individual scenes in various directions. For instance, contrasting olfactory perceptions could be employed to switch, break up, or reverse the order between individual pages in a picture book. By combining smells from various odour families – some calming and others uplifting – authors can set scenes with smells in the same way that images or music are used in digital books.

Moreover, smells can enhance the complexity of story characters. Instead of simply categorizing characters by bad or good smells, authors could introduce intriguing smells that add an extra dimension to a character, such as a protagonist with an unusual perfume, for example. By thoughtfully incorporating smells, authors can create richer, more immersive experiences for young readers and explore new narrative possibilities.

Expanding on these findings, we explored the history and types of scratch-and-sniff books (Spence et al., 2024). Scratch-and-sniff books are a fascinating reading experience that many will remember from their childhoods with distinct smells. In the quest to find out how many and what kinds of scratch-and-sniff books actually exist, we analysed popular titles and incorporated Jas Brooks' (2020) work, in which he purchased and smelled each book to determine the quality of the scents. We conducted a narrative historical review, beginning with a search for academic and peer-reviewed publications discussing scratch-and-sniff books. This initial search revealed only six relevant books, which did not align with the many scratch-and-sniff books published. Therefore, we extended our search to book databases, catalogues, and publishers' lists. This involved searching lists from popular online booksellers for all English-language book titles mentioning scratch-and-sniff. Through this extensive search, we located 245 items.

Our analysis revealed that the distribution of these books was heavily skewed towards young children. Adults' books with scratch-and-sniff surfaces exist but these tend to be artistic objects and poetry titles rather than fiction. For children, scratch-and-sniff books have typically twenty-six pages per book (shorter books for younger children) and the number of scents per book varies from seven, eight, and eleven scents on average for different age groups. The trend that the vast majority of scratch-and-sniff books (n=201, 82 per cent) are designed for young children (under eight years old) has been consistent across decades, with the number of such books increasing over time, from twenty books in the 1970s to fifty-seven in the 2010s, and already twenty-one books from 2020 to 2023, including two announced for publication in 2024.

As for the use of various smells in the books, we found that pleasant smells like cinnamon and chocolate dominate children's scratch-and-sniff picture books. There is a strong focus on categorizing smells as either good or bad, although we did find a few titles that deviate from this pattern and include the abstract nature of smells, using textual prompts or leading questions, such as "What does this smell feel like?" (which is expected to be followed by the reader scratching and sniffing a fragrance).

While popular books on Amazon's bestseller list, as reviewed by our earlier study (Kucirkova & Tosun, 2023), tend to use smell as an add-on feature for reader engagement, our historical review revealed that many older scratch-and-sniff books were crafted with smell as a central narrative or sensory element. This suggests that earlier books were of higher quality in terms of meaningfully integrating smell into the story narrative.

Adding smell to stories: beyond gimmick

The quality of children's books is crucial for a good reading experience and for smell to gain the place it deserves in literature, it must be more than a gimmick. Perhaps you disagree and may have kept a scratch-and-sniff book as your favourite book that simply contained smells as something different and novel back at the time. The invention of scratch-and-sniff dates to the 1960s, when Dr Gayle Matson, an organic chemist working on carbonless paper, made an unexpected discovery. He found that if tiny plastic beads containing encapsulated ink were spread onto a paper surface and then scratched with a fingernail, it created the illusion that the finger was writing like a pen. This happened because the pressure of the finger broke open the ink beads as it moved across the page. Matson then replaced the ink with fragrance, leading to the creation of the first scratch-and-sniff surface.

Several scratch-and-sniff stickers became popular, often linked to artificial fruit scents like strawberry or banana. Today, such stickers evoke nostalgic memories for many, including my parents. The scratch-and-sniff technique is experiencing a resurgence in popularity. For instance, while writing this book, the French postal service released a scented stamp issued by La Poste. This stamp depicts a baguette adorned with a red, white, and blue ribbon and features a "bakery scent", as described by the Parisian stationery shop Le Carré d'encre. This example highlights how popular culture can intersect with literature, bringing sensory experiences into everyday items and how scratch-and-sniff may act as an invitation to old and cherished practices – such as sending traditional mail.

The baguette-scented stamp also highlights the predominant use of smell and pictures: smell is added to match the picture rather than to augment it in any way. Researchers have criticized such a "pleonastic" use of smell, where a scent simply matches the odour of what is described or depicted. For instance, if a rabbit is eating a raspberry in a scene, a scratch-and-sniff surface might release a raspberry scent, which matches the picture but does not expand the meaning, thus misses the opportunity to augment the quality of a literary experience. Such gimmicky use of smell has been heavily criticized by filmmakers and live performance artists.

For example, the filmmaker Grace Boyle, who works with olfactory elements, argues that merely replicating a visually apparent scent is redundant. Banes (2001) suggested that in audiovisual representations, olfactory elements should be intentionally woven into the entire narrative from the beginning. This means incorporating smell meaningfully into the story or film, not as an afterthought but as an integral part of the script. Despite several calls to prioritize smell as an olfactory practice in its own right, smell is often regarded as less important than other senses, frequently being relegated to a secondary role in the creative process. This marginalization may hinder progress in the field, resulting in the use of smell in literature and media as gimmicky rather than substantive.

Smell in film and cinema

It is no secret that smell has been a neglected sense in media compared with sight and sound. While cinema and literature excel in visual and auditory storytelling, olfactory elements have been largely overlooked, with only sporadic attempts to incorporate them.

A prime example of how smell was introduced into the world of cinema was through Smellovision (initially called Scentovision), which premiered at the World's Fair in New York in 1939. Technologically, it was a new but basic concept, consisting mainly of a series of pipes attached to viewers' chairs through which a projectionist could deliver smells synchronized with the images being shown. While exciting because of its novelty, there were several issues with Scentovision's approach. The scents were too diffuse, inadequately calibrated in terms of intensity, and premature in terms of the research supporting the hedonic quality that most visitors would find appealing. As a result, Smellovision never took off and was written off in history as a failure of olfactory art. The case of Smellovision illustrates an instance where technology advanced ahead of research and was consequently considered a failure. Had researchers been central to the invention, it is unlikely that issues such as smell fatigue, subjective variations in scent preferences, and the drawbacks of pairing the same smell with the same image would have surfaced. Nevertheless, the example holds potential for improvement with increased collaboration between smell research and industry. That said, considerable challenges persist in olfactory experiences, whether in cinemas or theatres.

There are technical challenges to integrating various kinds of smells with the digital medium, but also social issues wherein smells may potentially evoke adverse reactions or discomfort without extensive prior testing. Notwithstanding, experimental efforts to incorporate smell into media continue and are particularly widespread in entertainment media. In various children's amusement parks around the world, smell machines release multiple types of scents related (or not) to the users' experience into the air. The olfactory company AromaPrime began with scent machines in Disney parks and has since specialized in amusement parks for children, creating scents connected to various favourite children's stories. Today, AromaPrime offers a variety of ready-made smells that can enhance an amusement park adventure. This isn't the scent marketing you would encounter in a luxurious hotel; these are scent machines with smells such as those found in award-winning Halloween haunts and multisensory museum experiences. The selection of scents includes scene-setting smells, such as "smugglers' cave", "burnt gunpowder", "dragon smoke", and "unicorn". These scents seem more aligned with the fantasy worlds that our children commented on when we interviewed them about the smells within their stories. Interestingly too, these scents are not the kinds of scents we had found in our review of scratch-and-sniff books on the market, which often feature rather mundane smells that merely repeat the depicted objects on the page.

The question of whether smell will become more prevalent in films and literature in the future is open to speculation. Advancements in technology may eventually make it more feasible and affordable to incorporate olfactory elements into storytelling. Additionally, as audiences crave more immersive experiences, there could be a growing demand for multisensory narratives that engage multiple senses simultaneously. I believe that to elevate the role of smell in literature, it must be thoughtfully integrated from the outset, enhancing the narrative and providing a richer, more immersive experience. This shift in approach is essential for smell to be recognized as a significant and valuable sensory element in storytelling.

Smell in children's literature

A prime example of how to incorporate smell into children's literature without making it a gimmick, is the beloved book *Stellaluna* by Janell Cannon (published by Clarion Books in 1993). The story follows a young fruit bat named Stellaluna who becomes separated from her mother and ends up with a nest of birds. Raised by the birds, Stellaluna learns to behave like them. However, a crucial moment in the story occurs when Stellaluna's mother recognizes her through smell. This emphasizes the importance of maternal scent in bringing characters together. *Stellaluna* beautifully weaves this olfactory ability into the narrative, making it a standout example of how to incorporate sensory elements into a delightful children's book.

One thing is to include smell into the narrative (rather than to make smell merely repeat illustrated objects). Another thing altogether is the technical side of including smell in children's books. On the practical side, it is crucial to ensure that when smell is integrated into literature, it does not overwhelm the reader, leading to "olfactory overload" (unwanted, overly strong odours or the accumulation of scents in a space). Just as with other senses, sensory overload can occur with smell – too many fast-moving bright images, loud music, or multiple scents in a confined space, such as perfumeries in airports, can overwhelm sensitive noses.

People have different thresholds for what constitutes overload, so what may be tolerable for one reader might be overwhelming for another. One of the best ways to avoid this is to give readers control. Mechanistically, this means that odours in scratch-and-sniff books should be released only when activated by the reader. By controlling the intensity of scratching and the frequency of doing so, or by placing their nose close to the fra-granced surface, readers can manage how much odour is released. Theo-retically, providing readers with control over the sensory stimuli they encounter aligns with the concept of agency and the extensive literature on the importance of agency in reading and engagement with educational technology (Brod et al., 2024). Agency, in this context, refers to the ability of readers to manage and influence their own reading experience. By allowing readers to control the release of scents, we respect their sensory preferences and enhance their engagement with the material. This approach not only improves the reading experience but also supports a more thoughtful and intentional integration of smell into literature.

Agency in olfactory reading

In my project "Sensory Books", colleagues and I examined how parents and children exercise their agency when reading scratch-and-sniff books together at home. Specifically, we observed who initiates the scratching of the scented surface and how this interaction influences the shared reading experience. Our first study involved ten families with children aged between three and five years, all native Norwegian speakers. The families were instructed to engage in book reading "as they normally would at home", and we provided them with a scratch-and-sniff book, *Peter Follows His Nose* by Beatrix Potter. This book features a rabbit named Peter, who navigates his environment by smelling and tasting various foods and herbs, such as lavender, strawberries, mushrooms, and onions. Each page contains a fragranced area that releases a scent corresponding to the depicted item when scratched (pleonastic use). We analysed videotaped reading sessions of families with this scratch-and-sniff book, as well as two other books: the child's favourite book, selected by the family from their home library, and a comparison book provided to the parents, *A Fly Flew* by Sondre Lerch (2021), a popular children's book.

Our qualitative analysis focused on understanding how the fragranced surfaces in the scratch-and-sniff book engaged both parents and children in the reading experience. We analysed whether the act of scratching the surface was predominantly initiated by the parent, the child, or collaboratively. Additionally, we compared the engagement and interaction patterns with those observed during the reading of the child's favourite book and the comparison book. This approach allowed us to explore the dynamics of sensory engagement and the role of olfactory elements in enhancing the reading experience for young children and their parents.

We found that both children and parents used their noses, fingers, hands, and heads in different ways when exploring the scents in the scratch-and-sniff book. Some families sniffed the scents quickly, while others took their time. The families used different techniques like scratching, sniffing, and waving the book to catch the smells. We also noticed that the way adults and children reacted to the smells varied a lot. Sometimes they were completely in sync, and other times they weren't. Touch, sight, and smell were the senses that were most involved in the reading experience.

Taken together, the study findings suggest that olfaction can serve as a means to establish joint attention between adults and children, complementing and enhancing other attention-soliciting elements of books, such as illustrations. Given the positive atmosphere connected to the reading of the scratch-and-sniff books, we recommend incorporating olfaction into the practice of shared book reading. This approach can facilitate bonding between adult and young readers that is not solely based on language and as such, offer a new avenue in book reading, which has been, naturally, dominated by the linguistic focus.

Having explored the ways in which olfaction has been incorporated into children's books and probed questions of how it could be integrated into new children's book titles in the future, the next step in our project was to explore the actual engagement of children when reading books with added smells. The scratch-and-sniff study with parents at home showed us some interaction patterns we can expect with scratch-and-sniff books that contain smells merely added to the illustrations. But what about interactions with books where smell is intentionally included as part of the plot, as an abstract quality that takes children to augmented dimensions, going beyond the pleonastic use? Will it still engage the young readers?

Smell in reading engagement

To address this inquiry, our first task was to identify a book that could provide children with an immersive olfactory reading experience, and then devise an experiment around it. The children's literature market offers several intriguing titles exploring the sense of smell. Alongside our systematic reviews, we considered Margaret Hyde's series of six books, beginning with *Mo Smells Red* (2008) and concluding with *Mo Smells Pink* (2011). These books utilize safe, hypoallergenic essential oils and employ a "Press 2 Smell" technology, developed by Hyde, which retains the scent until activated by pressing and can be used up to 150,000 times – making it suitable for our experiment.

However, while children's literature often incorporates smells for humour, such as strong or unpleasant odours that appeal to young readers, there is a noticeable lack of books dedicated to exploring subtle and abstract scents, which are integral to everyday olfactory experiences. In adult fiction, we're familiar with novels featuring "Supersmellers", such as Grenouille in Patrick Suskind's *Perfume.* While this concept has been used in children's stories, we sought a narrative where smell is seamlessly integrated into the story, similar to how music complements a plot. As such a book wasn't readily available, we decided to create one by collaborating with a professional children's author and an olfactory artist.

After navigating through various twists and turns, we arrived at a book that wasn't exactly what we had initially envisioned, but it served as a prototype for testing children's responses. This book was presented to children on an iPad and featured moments in the story that corresponded to one of four distinct smells. These smells were physically available to the children in the form of four canisters, which they were prompted to open and sniff at specific points in the narrative. The scents were sourced from the board game "Les boîtes a`odeurs"

(Nature & Decouvertes Ltd) and were carefully chosen to have similar intensity and quality, enhancing the story without being explicitly mentioned in the text. The smells followed a pattern of positive–neutral–negative–positive valence. With our testing protocol established (Løkken et al., 2023), we embarked on an experimental study with children in Norwegian kindergartens.

In this experiment, we utilized three books: a traditional paper-based book and two specially designed digital books that we had created. Both digital books were designed to be read either with or without olfaction enhancement, which involved the manipulation of the canisters by the children. All three books were similar in terms of length, pacing, and complexity. To assess whether children learned more words from interacting with these books with or without smell, we included a set of target vocabulary words in the two digital books. These words were selected to be unfamiliar to a typical five-year-old and of comparable difficulty across the books.

Since this was an experiment rather than a qualitative observation study like the one involving families reading scratch and sniff books at home, the fieldworker/researcher followed a structured procedure. Each book was read twice to each child over a period of three days, with the order of the digital books and the olfaction enhancement of one book randomly assigned. To assess the effects of the books on children's outcomes, tests of story recall and vocabulary were administered by the researcher after the second reading of each book. These reading and testing sessions were conducted one-to-one in a quiet space within the kindergartens. The participants in this study were sixty-five Norwegian-speaking children aged between four and five years old, with no language-based special education needs. Children were recruited from kindergartens located in two municipalities in the southeast of Norway.

After analysing the results from the tests statistically and coding the videos comprehensively, we found that there was no direct relationship between olfactory stimulation, vocabulary acquisition, and reading comprehension. What we did find was a relationship between children's engagement and the olfactory enhancement of stories. The participating children were more engaged with the story when exposed to olfactory stimuli (target condition) compared with when there were no olfactory stimuli (control condition). Specifically, the results showed significant increases in various engagement metrics. Engagement was measured using a scale ranging from 1 to 7, where 7 indicated the highest level of engagement. We focused on three subscales of engagement, which were adapted from previous reading studies.

First, we assessed persistence, which reflects the child's active involvement and goal-directed behaviour throughout the reading session.

This included actions such as pointing at pictures and words, turning pages, making positive comments about the book, and asking questions. Second, we looked at enthusiasm, which captures the child's expressive engagement, vitality, and eagerness displayed during the reading session. This was observed through indicators of enjoyment, such as smiling, laughing, showing genuine interest, and demonstrating eagerness to continue reading.

Lastly, we considered compliance, which indicates the child's willingness to cooperate during the reading session by following the adult's instructions, responding to questions, and meeting the expectations of the activity.

In our analysis of engagement, we also considered children's facial responses to gain deeper insights into their level of engagement. What we discovered was not surprising: the introduction of olfactory cues significantly enhanced children's engagement with digital books. Specifically, when the books were read with the inclusion of olfactory canisters containing scents, there were statistically significant increases in children's persistence, enthusiasm, compliance, overall engagement, and facial responses during the reading sessions.

These are important findings as they could inspire new approaches for motivating children to read. Persistence in engagement is particularly noteworthy as it aligns with the goal of reading to keep children engaged for longer periods. Introducing smell into reading may serve as a strategy to capture the interest of reluctant readers and increase overall reading engagement. These findings carry positive practical implications but it is important to note that they do not directly correlate with learning outcomes such as improved reading comprehension or vocabulary acquisition. Whether heightened engagement resulting from reading books enhanced with smell can lead to these outcomes remains an unanswered question that warrants further investigation through additional experiments or longitudinal studies.

Our findings align with previous experimental research with young children and smell. In one key study in the United States, Epple and Herz (1999) tested an important hypothesis: previous research with adults has demonstrated that once smells become linked to certain emotions, it is hard to change or forget those associations. From this, the researchers extrapolated that smells can be connected to emotions through learning and this can affect children's behaviour. They found that this is true in an experiment. Twenty-four boys and twenty-four girls, all five years old, were given a tricky maze to solve while being exposed to a hidden smell. After finishing the maze, they moved to another room for a tough thinking task. Some children were in a room with the same smell as the maze, some had a different smell, and some had no smell at all.

The children who had the same smell from the maze in the second task scored lower than the others. The researchers chose to use a negative emotional situation to see how it affected the results but they recommend that also positive situations, like feeling successful are tested with smell, as this could improve performance or motivation on a thinking task.

Overall, these results showed that emotions linked to smells can affect how we behave. If a smell is connected to failure, it can make it harder to do well on a tricky task afterward. This notion has significant implications for places where smells can be controlled, such as schools or homes or public spaces like libraries. Imagine being more intentional in terms of the smells children are exposed to and how, consequently, these environments influence children's responses and associations with a reading experience, for example.

Smell and interactivity

It is a common critique that adding olfactory elements to books simply enhances interactivity and that increased interactivity is what ultimately drives engagement. This notion is evident in all the testing scenarios we've explored in our project, from scratch-and-sniff books to interactive exhibitions where children open boxes or canisters with smells. To address this criticism and delve deeper into the impact of olfactory stimuli on reading engagement, I am currently investigating the effects of ambient smells on adult readers in Finland.

In this experiment, participants are exposed to either pleasant fresh ocean scents or unpleasant odours while reading. By observing how these different smells affect the readers' engagement with the text, we hope to uncover valuable insights. Will the unpleasant smell deter them from reading altogether, or will they become more focused when surrounded by pleasant scents, leading to better recall of the story? There are countless variations of this experiment that we can explore to better understand the multifaceted ways in which smell influences the reading experience.

Our prediction is that the ambient smell will influence the readers' behaviour and reading experience, although we don't know in which direction. Several consumer research studies show that subliminal odours – odours released in the environment where adults interact – can influence behaviour. Consumer research with adults shows for example that it can increase purchasing behaviour in terms of spending more money but also more time in shopping malls and restaurants with pleasant smells (Sela & Sobel, 2010). Not surprising then that McDonald's, the world's largest fast food restaurant chain, uses in its marketing scented billboards that smell like its French fries. Scented billboards or aromas diffused around shopping malls are not for users to interact with. In contrast, when it comes to reading and literacy, the interactivity of the object with the reader is a crucial component of the experience and the reader behaviour. Interactivity is typically achieved through touch and haptic reading experiences, which warrant special attention in children's reading.

Touch and smell in children's books

Interactivity of books is not a unified concept in terms of how it is studied in literacy research, often being confined to interaction through touch and the physical engagement of hands with books. Touch is an important way of finding one's way in the story and incorporating the body as part of the reading experience. My colleague at the University of Stavanger, Professor Anne Mangen, has specifically researched how crucial hands are in navigating lengthy literary novels and how this aids in story comprehension. In children's literature, various types of haptic engagement exist, such as pop-up, lift-the-flap, touch-and-feel books, allowing children to explore through hands and fingers, touching different surfaces and engaging in various types of tactile interactions. Often in children's books, these interactions involve feeling animal fur or the flat surface of a mirror. Scratch-and-sniff books are considered a separate category from such tactile interactive children's books. In this respect it is worth noting that while in English we distinguish between books that are tactile only and books that are tactile with an olfactory surface – scratch-and-sniff books – this is not a common distinction in Japanese, where "shikake ehon" encompasses all books that have some kind of "trick" in them, engaging readers through additional senses beyond just visual.

In addition to engagement and text navigation, touch (as in the possibility of directly touching text in relation to specific story characters in digital books) was hypothesized to increase readers' empathy (Zhao & Unsworth, 2016). The researchers speculated that readers would feel a closer connection to the book characters if they could directly touch them. Certainly, in terms of the distance between the reader and the story character, touching the characters on the digital book page reduces the distance. Would adding olfactory qualities to the story characters further reduce the distance? In this state of the art research field, we don't know, but theoretically we can assume so. In print or analogue books with tactile features, the combination of touch and smell is recognized as an important mechanism for engaging readers.

Research on visually impaired children shows that tactile illustrations are beneficial for the language and literacy development of children with blindness or low vision (Heller & Gentaz, 2014). Stratton and Wright (1991) argue that tactile illustrations help visually impaired children understand and remember stories. Work by Klatzky and colleagues indicates that touch is useful for processing the material properties of books but not their spatial properties. It is texture that supports the identification of 3D objects (e.g. Klatzky et al., 1985; 1993). Therefore, perhaps the ideal book for children with smell would be one presented in textured 3D formats, ensuring that the design is inclusive for all types of readers.

Researchers are delving into why readers seem more engaged when scent is involved, probing the underlying mechanisms. Could it be the element of surprise, catching them off guard and drawing them in? Or perhaps it's the heightened attention sparked by emotional stimulation? My bet is on mood – the connection between smell and emotional states – as the driving force behind reader engagement. Though I haven't directly studied this with children, research with adult readers suggests that pleasant scents lead to longer focus on specific objects or images and overall improved mood (Knasko, 1995). It must be acknowledged here that, as Spence (2020) caveats, scents' impact on mood and well-being hinges on multisensory congruency – if other sensory inputs, like music, clash with olfactory stimulation, the effect may be diminished. It is when there is harmony among sensory experiences that the olfactory environment in our surroundings can profoundly influence our mood and the reading experience.

Embodied olfactory experiences

Returning to the concept of agency and prioritizing child-centred methods, I have been inspired by various community-oriented projects in France that actively involve children and smell into their practices. For example, in 2022, OsmoArt, in collaboration with "The sea through the five senses" organized by the Cannes Orchestra, created an exhibition that focused on marine notes and perfumes revolving around the theme of the sea with an olfactory animation where they involved schoolchildren. On an ongoing basis in the Smell Lab museum in Berlin, olfactory artists teach a course on smells and scents to children between ten and fifteen years old, including those with and without migration backgrounds. Using different fragrances, the course aims not only to evoke emotions associated with home but also to foster an environment with awareness of various essential oils among the children.

I have also drawn inspiration from critical scholars who emphasize power dynamics in their research and urge us to pause and reflect before jumping onto olfactory activities. These scholars have prompted me to reconsider certain approaches as I explore various methods. Notably, Biswas (2021) underscores the importance of recognizing power dynamics between adults and children in classrooms and encourages us to consider how both parties can act as teachers, revealing alternative ways of perceiving and existing in the world. Biswas' work reminds researchers that it is crucial to be mindful of "childism" in shaping the field of olfactory research with children, respecting children as individuals with their own experiences and perspectives. Childism makes it clear that, despite the responsibility to guide and care for children, it is essential to recognize that adults do not have ownership over them. Children possess agency and contribute their own insights on how olfaction influences their narratives. So, when creating an olfactory exhibition or course for children, one needs to seriously ask: is this an activity for the children or for the adults? Who initiated it and who benefits?

This is where I envision the potential for art to serve as a platform for fostering new approaches that enable adults and children to connect and explore diverse understandings of olfaction, both despite and because of their power differences. Stories, in particular, can serve as powerful catalysts for creating these shared spaces of encounter. In my early research, I delved into stories crafted by children and parents using the Our Story app on iPads, an open-ended platform developed during my PhD at the Open University in England. Unlike traditional templates-based story apps, Our Story allows users to combine images, sounds, and texts to create multimedia narratives that can be shared with others.

What I gleaned from this research, and what I now bring to my work with olfaction, is the importance of a prolonged exploratory and iterative phase before translating research findings into tangible resources for children. While it may be tempting to assume that teachers swiftly incorporate abstract smells into children's stories en masse based on research insights, it is essential to proceed with caution. I've been approached by numerous publishers eager to enhance their titles with various scent diffusers and scratch-and-sniff surfaces. However, we must consider whether such enhancements truly align with children's interests and needs or if they merely reflect adults' desire to engage children in what adults deem desirable experiences.

Agentic olfactory experiences

My current approach is guided by the work of multisensory scholars who frequently collaborate with artists in their exploratory studies. One such scholar is Professor Jennifer Rowsell, who has consistently embraced a collaborative ethos in her research, involving artists, app developers, and various community members. Her work on literacy underscores the significance of relationships, both material and social, with agency serving as a cornerstone of inclusive practices. Alongside Professor Kate Pahl, Rowsell introduced the concept of artifactual critical literacy, highlighting the intersection of material cultural studies and critical literacy education (Pahl & Rowsell, 2013). The notion of "living literacies", as discussed by these scholars, emphasizes that stories, whether in print or digital form, accompanied by sounds or haptic experiences, are experienced and embodied in everyday life across diverse spaces and populations, sustaining diversity and ensuring longevity (Pahl & Rowsell, 2020).

Scratch-and-sniff books are an excellent way to illustrate the theoretical concepts of living and artifactual literacies. These books utilize scratch-and-sniff technology, which is also present in everyday objects like magazine fragrance samples and scented stickers that come with their own stories. Often, these books serve as artifacts, evoking nostalgia for adults who remember their childhood experiences with them and creating happy memories for children reading with their parents at home. It is the context that the memory of reading returns to.

The Proustian effect, where the author Marcel Proust dipped a madeleine in his tea, is often cited to illustrate the connection between memory and olfaction. Indeed, the "madeleine episode" has become such a cultural touchstone for the smell-memory experience that Gilbert (2008) wrote that: "psychologists have made Proust their mascot for smell memory" (p. 190). The Proustian example, however, also underscores the importance of adult perspectives on smell in reading as an adult way back to childhood. The madeleine's scent evoked vivid memories for Proust, but that doesn't mean that this is a universal experience. Context matters hugely when it comes to literacy and literary experiences.

Cathy Burnett and other new literacy scholars stress that literacy cannot be divorced from its contextual setting (Burnett et al., 2014b). Different social and cultural groups have different approaches to reading and writing and the context in which literacy "happens". Burnett and colleagues emphasize that context shapes and is shaped by various identities and experiences of learners. Keeping this scholarship in mind is crucial as we collectively figure out an emerging field of olfactory literacies, developing unique methods and areas of focus.

One approach I've been exploring to understand children's responses, without necessarily imposing my adult set of expectations, is through subtle aromatic changes in children's environments. For instance, at a local library in Stavanger, children participate in the Saga Writing League. During these sessions, they are provided with writing materials and support from volunteers who assist the children in crafting their stories. The stories are then printed and made available for borrowing from the library. What makes this project unique is its emphasis on children's agency and letting them create and own their stories. Following my recommendation, the library staff added a subtle aroma of bergamot in the background for the writing sessions, diffused through air diffusers.

Will children who write with bergamot wafting above them produce more stories than children without? Will the aroma influence the content or literary quality of their stories in any way? Would another aroma, for example vanilla, produce different results? Would this be different for younger children? And is there a difference between boys and girls, children with and without attentional difficulties, children with and without language delays?

To answer detailed questions about the effectiveness of olfaction in literacy, we require numerous additional studies. It is unlikely that merely adding drops of bergamot essential oil drastically alters children's writing. But it might be that adding bergamot will enhance the creative atmosphere for the children as they conjure up their stories. As we are more and more integrating smell into sensory literacies, we can explore these and other questions, the answers of which will shape future literacy experiences.

5 Cultural and socio-technical influences on olfaction

Perfumery is a relatively slow industry to innovate. Historically, master perfumers, known as "noses", were the ones who selected a range of key scent elements and precise technical specifications for upcoming fragrances. They had their own secret recipes for meticulous evaluation notes, combinations, intensities, and dilutions for the final perfume that only they could create. Consequently, there is a lot of resistance among artisan perfumers and master perfumers to having their craft replaced by AI-generated formulas. However, whether we like it or not, AI is enhancing the time-consuming process of fragrance creation. Numerous fragrance brands now leverage biometric research combined with generative AI and machine learning algorithms to develop scents that can evoke emotional reactions and make us feel good.

Few realize the extent of materials and the space these historically occupied in perfume houses. American perfumer Mandy Aftel, renowned as the owner and nose behind the natural perfume line Aftelier, showcases this in panoramic old photographs exhibited at her house. These images reveal the substantial space that was required to store natural ingredients and extracts from animals or plants. Today, thanks to technological advancements, the storage space is significantly minimized, reflecting the transfer of already distilled molecules. The allure of perfumery has definitely not diminished over the years, though, with the current perfumery industry estimated to reach USD 64.41 billion by 2030.

Perfumery

People have various preferences for where they apply perfumes – such as the neck, hair, underarms, earlobes, cleavage, or wrists – and how often they use perfume, which can vary by purpose or occasion. But what really is a perfume?

Perfume is a complex composition of multiple ingredients, often consisting of more than a hundred components. To illustrate, let's take

DOI: 10.4324/9781003482024-5

the iconic example of Chanel No. 5, known as the "timeless, legendary fragrance" (Chanel.com, n.d.), that revolutionized the perfumery industry when it was developed in 1921. While most perfumes of that era were based on a single floral note, Chanel No. 5 distinguished itself by creating a fragrance that embodied the essence of a "woman". Achieving this required a complex composition of several notes.

One key innovation introduced by Chanel No. 5 was the use of aldehydes, fatty compounds that impart an elusive, almost lemony quality to the fragrance. Aldehydes have the ability to lift a fragrance, offsetting the sweetness and heaviness of other ingredients. Key raw materials in Chanel No. 5 include rose centifolia, jasmine, and ylang-ylang, along with other components such as orris root, iris root, and natural musks. In total, Chanel No. 5 is crafted from more than eighty ingredients (Mohammed et al., 2021), resulting in a multilayered formulation that has captivated generations.

To grasp the intricate composition of Chanel No. 5, the artist Maki Ueda (2012) explored the breakdown of its individual notes in her project "olfactoscape". Ueda strategically placed or sprayed the aromatic ingredients of Chanel No. 5 in various locations, allowing visitors to experience each tone independently before encountering the full perfume. This process of deconstruction and reconstruction vividly illustrates the complexity of ingredients and craftsmanship behind a single sniff of a perfume. I like the choice of the word "scape" in Ueda's exhibition. A "scape" implies a scenery or space where perfumes and odours unfold, highlighting how our awareness of scent environments, and the navigation thereof, are deeply influenced by culture.

Perfumes across cultures

Perfumes are used across cultures, whether commercially produced or homemade, with various values attached to them. While France is often described as the capital of perfume, historically, Egypt holds this distinction and I guess that even the most devoted French alchemist would admit that the history of making scents begins with Egypt. It was in Egypt where the development of manufacturing techniques for incense, cosmetics, and perfumery catered to a range of spiritual and social aromatic occasions.

Egyptian cosmetic care was frequently focused on protecting the skin from the sun's harsh rays. One method involved placing a solidified cone of scented beef tallow on the top of the head. As the day progressed, the unguent would gradually melt, covering the hair and body with a film of fragrance (Fletcher, 1998). Egyptian perfumes were a very precious commodity, reserved for three specific purposes: the aesthetic needs of the very rich and royal class, offerings to deities, and embalming the dead. A lot has changed since – today, perfumes are used by the poor and rich, the old and young.

Perfumes and children are often discussed within a protection discourse, suggesting that children should not be exposed to perfumes or that there should be a specific age from which children can safely use them. Perfumes and children are also frequently discussed in terms of gender: girls are often thought to respond more sophisticatedly and discerningly to various types of odours, a trait attributed to their more frequent play with perfumes compared with boys. As mentioned in the previous chapter, girls' greater odour discrimination indicates a cultural influence not an inborn difference and it is exposure to various odours that influences their ability to perceive and name them.

That said, in addition to cultural factors, there is also a genetic component that affects olfactory perception and preference: Mallet and Schaal (1998) tested nine-year-old children for their perception and memory of their peers' odours. The researchers investigated the intriguing possibility that olfactory memory plays a role in the emotional regulation of friendships. They hypothesized that the opportunity children have to memorize the individual olfactory properties of their classmates influences how they select and maintain friendships.

To test this, odours were sampled from cotton t-shirts worn next to the skin by a group of children for four consecutive nights and the entire day preceding the tests. Another group of children smelled these t-shirts, and were asked to rate the pleasantness of the smells, attribute the smell to either boys or girls, and recognize who the smell belonged to. No perfume was allowed in the experiment.

The findings revealed that these nine-year-old children recognized their peers by odour better than by chance. The raters consistently perceived the girls' odours as more pleasant and perfumed than the boys'. The researchers noted that the lower pleasantness and "perfumedness" of boys' odours might reinforce their self-perception as males, thereby supporting the endorsement of typical gender roles, such as being "active and strong".

The study by Mallet and Schaal (1998) provides an intriguing possibility that smell plays a much more important role in friendships from an early age than previously assumed. This role is often overlooked because experimental brain research shows that subliminal smells exert a profound influence on human behaviour and perception (Sela & Sobel, 2010). I find the research fascinating because emerging research suggests that odours are implicated in face perception in infants and this has important social implications. Several studies have shown that body odours with high social relevance for infants, such as the odour emanating from the mother, influence how infants categorize faces among other objects, their face-scanning behaviour, and their perception of facial expressions (Damon et al., 2021). There is thus much more to odour and children's natural behaviour than we know of.

Body odours undergo changes throughout development, impacting interpersonal communication between parents and their children. Research by Croy et al. (2017), based on a questionnaire with Polish parents, revealed that babies are perceived as smelling wonderful to their parents, whereas teenagers are not. Recent findings by Owsienko et al. (2024b) shed light on the molecular basis of this phenomenon, attributing it to sexual maturation coinciding with changes in body odour chemical composition. Post-pubescent teens exhibit notes of sweat, urine, cheese, and goat in their body odour samples, contrasting with the essences of lilac and raspberry detected in samples from babies. As children approach adolescence, their scents undergo a dramatic transformation due to the activation of sweat glands, likely serving evolutionary and communicative purposes (Owsienko et al., 2024a). No wonder that "baby powder diffusers" are among the best sellers in online shops!

Perfumes are traditionally considered an adult commodity, but they are increasingly entering the childhood world. This varies across different cultures; for example, in Cuba, it is common for children to use perfumes, whereas in Norway, children are typically prohibited from using them. When you look up "baby perfume" in international online shops, you will find a large collection of fragrances and sprays specially developed for infants, with some themed in popular children's stories or characters (e.g. Peppa Pig eau de cologne). These are advertised for direct application to children's skin and are intended to attract parents with a pleasant aroma of their babies. While shampoos and soaps for children are often fragrance-free or contain fragrances in very low concentrations, fragrances and toy cosmetics can be a different story. These products often contain ingredients that exceed safety guidelines, exposing children to well-known allergens at concentrations considered unsafe (Rastogi et al., 1999). Given the significance of babies' natural smells for fostering bonding between parents and children, I align with the scientists who discourage the use of perfume and fragranced products with infants.

One fascinating aspect of studying olfaction is its duality: it can be concrete when discussing specific applications such as products for babies, yet elusive and abstract when it comes to verbalizing and understanding smells. We use smell to navigate our contexts and bond with others in a subliminal, emotion-led manner, akin to abstract concepts like time or space. A single puff of perfume can instantly transport us to a memory of an ex-lover, completely uprooting us from our current reality.

Perhaps the quickest entry into the cultural appreciation of smell is through the examination of the various words associated with smell. I am a French and Spanish speaker and have often wondered how the French term for smell, *sentir*, and the Spanish *saber*, both of which come from the Latin *sentire*, meaning to perceive, might be related to *el sabor* or *la saveur*, which are about flavour and semantically related to the Latin *sapio*, meaning to perceive precisely, to know. Perhaps these etymological connections reveal that *to smell is to know*.

My Japanese classes were only at a basic level, but I have learned that there are multiple words for various kinds of smelling behaviour which we don't have in English. For example, there is a distinction in Japanese between the receiver and the emitter of a smell. Japanese also have their own word for the smell of asphalt after rain, often referred to in English as petrichor, which is the earthy scent produced when rain falls on dry soil.

Some languages possess richer olfactory vocabularies and engage in more frequent discussions of smell than others (e.g. Majid, 2021). Majid's (2021) review revealed that smell vocabulary is not only limited but also that references to smells are very infrequent. She cites an example from a linguistic analysis of written textual sources relevant to the 2,000 km^2 area in the north-west of England – the Lake District National Park. The researchers' analysis included corpus creation and extraction, classification, and georeferencing of first-person descriptions of sights, sounds, and smells. Their analysis of almost 8 million words from 7,000 British English texts containing first-person descriptions of the Lake District found 28,445 descriptions referring to sight, 1,480 descriptions of sound experiences, and only 78 descriptions of smells (Koblet & Purves, 2020). So, at least in English, we can safely conclude that not only are there relatively few smell words to begin with, but also that these are not much used. Could this be changed as we conduct more research across cultures with attention to smell?

Debunking some cultural myths about smell

In my research for this book, I delved into several popular books, blogs, multimedia materials, fragrance courses, and olfactory exhibitions. This range of sources is rather unusual for an academic, but it becomes self-explanatory when we consider how little published research literature exists on smell. Furthermore, olfactory studies are practically non-existent in traditional educational curricula, and there is no dedicated teaching of olfaction in schools. Not surprisingly then, much of the knowledge individuals possess about smell is self-taught and acquired through eclectic learning from others and various fragmented sources. Consequently, numerous myths, beliefs, and traditions persist.

Popular smell-related myths

One popular myth around smell is the notion that gender alone determines smell ability or that all children are inherently super-smellers. The reality is far more nuanced.

One important myth that has been debunked by repeated research is that different cultures have different smells or that different ethnic groups smell different because of their genes or different sweat glands. The truth is that eccrine sweat, which is a sweat gland present in almost all regions of the skin, carries the smell of various foods and spices consumed. So, if you smell a difference between groups of people it is very likely due to the food they consume (Herz, 2009).

Body odours are often tabooed and not discussed with children, or, if they are, it is usually about how to eliminate bad odours. However, body odours can actually be used to debunk myths about who smells good or bad and to foster acceptance of others. Professional olfactory specialists emphasize that nothing inherently smells bad; it is all in our perception. Odours play a crucial role in both self-acceptance and non-verbal communication (Diaconu, 2022), and this should be part of everyday discussions. Smelling others is a very intimate experience of fellow humans, especially as our environments become increasingly digitized and populated by "superhumans and posthumans" who are almost odourless. Artists explore this paradox through various installations aimed at shocking visitors with unpleasant odours like sweat or unwashed feet. These exhibitions highlight how seldom we collectively address the human aspect of smell, showcasing our reluctance to accept and discuss this fundamental part of our perception.

Another myth is that smoking damages the sense of smell. A comprehensive study conducted with 1,387 volunteers in Sweden by Brämerson et al. (2004) revealed that smell ability is influenced by multiple factors, including gender, age, and the presence of nasal polyps. However, gender and smoking were not identified as significant factors in the study, while nasal polyps emerged as a notable risk factor. This highlights the importance of considering various factors beyond smoking when exploring individual smell ability.

One such factor is personality traits, as shown in a recent analysis by Tyagi et al. (2024). The researchers analysed the responses to odours and the traits of 207 adult volunteers. They then conducted a detailed analysis to explore how personality traits and gender influence the ability to identify and distinguish between smells, and how these abilities relate to the perceived intensity, pleasantness, and familiarity of different odours. The results showed some connections between gender, personality traits, and the ability to tell apart and recognize smells, but not with simply detecting them. Specifically, people who scored high in conscientiousness and openness to experience were better at identifying smells. Participants who were more agreeable and conscientious (according to the personality test) were better at distinguishing between different smells. On the other hand, people with high extroversion scores tended to be worse at distinguishing smells. Additionally, as in other gender research, male participants were better at identifying smells, while female participants were better at distinguishing between different smells. The study highlights the important nuances not only in the connection between gender and individual characteristics in smell but also how responses are studied (odour differentiation is different from odour identification).

Cultural practices, traditions, and values significantly influence how we perceive, describe, and use smells. Reflecting on my role in olfactory research, I'm reminded of an important insight highlighted by Henrich, Heine, and Norenzayan in 2010. They noted a limitation in Western and scientific viewpoints: the tendency to exclusively focus on populations in "WEIRD" countries (Western, Educated, Industrialized, Rich, and Democratic). This narrow approach assumes that studying these populations can unveil universal truths about human nature and behaviour.

I want to clearly acknowledge this bias and let this acknowledgement not only frame the context for this book but also underscore the importance of recognizing the constraints of my own perspective. By acknowledging the limitations of our own experiences and cultural background, we need to embrace diverse perspectives beyond the confines of the WEIRD paradigm. Of course, the WEIRD limitation isn't unique to olfactory research – it applies across most studies in English-language literature. Researchers, including myself, often focus on typical "perfume countries" like France, Egypt, or Japan due to higher reporting rates, convenience, and access to cultural materials. However, this selective approach overlooks countless other cultural practices related to olfaction, limiting our understanding of its broader cultural significance.

With this caveat in mind, I want to propose that the relationship between smell and culture is direct: odours that unite a community become ingrained in their cultural fabric, signifying belonging and shared identity. The phenomenon, termed "collective olfactory memory" by Verbeek and Van Campen (2013), serves to bond people together or evoke feelings of belonging by tapping into the unique olfactory experiences of each region, nation, and subculture.

Collective olfactory memories

My own experiences moving across countries during my childhood and early adulthood, as well as conducting olfactory research in diverse cultural contexts like Malawi and Malta, have underscored that collective olfactory memories are real. If we define culture as the customs and artifacts that characterize a group of people in a certain geographical location, then we can find several culturally preferred smells. For example, the preferred smell of toilet cleaners in Norway is pine, while in Slovakia it is lemon, and in the United States it is more flowery vanilla fragrances. When you ask people about their favourite smells, their responses are likely to vary significantly between countries, yet within each culture there might be a notable consensus. If nothing else, you are likely to hear across cultures that vanilla smells nice because vanilla is also in research described as a universally liked scent (Spence, 2022).

During my visit to Valetta in Malta, as part of my visiting professorship at the Centre for Literacy Studies, I queried a group of Maltese students – future early childhood practitioners – about their favourite smells. They cited pastizzi, a greasy pastry, and sourdough, both of which held positive associations with food. Interestingly, garlic also garnered positive sentiments, while the scent of frankincense was considered neutral, perhaps due to the frequent exposure to this scent in churches (and its religious significance in Maltese society).

Additionally, amidst Malta's rapid urban development characterized by construction, pollution, and road closures, the smell of fresh tarmac emerged as a negative olfactory cue for this group of teacher-students. This illustrates how smells can reflect not only cultural preferences but also societal changes and challenges within a given socio-cultural context.

It is often said that, just as there are distinct genres in music like oriental or western, there are also recognizable scent profiles associated with different cultures. Each culture, and even individual countries, have their own signature smells that serve as cultural markers. For example, nearly every culture has a dish with a distinctive, pungent smell. Enjoying these odours can sometimes even signal one's membership to a particular culture, especially for immigrants.

As someone who was born in Slovakia and now lives in Norway, I often find myself reflecting on my own sense of cultural belonging based on my reaction to certain smells. For instance, traditional Slovakian fermented sheep cheese dumplings, "Brynzove Halusky", and the Norwegian fish "Lutefisk", both renowned for their strong bad smells are odours that I personally find off-putting. Yet, despite not enjoying the smells of my native Slovakia or adopted Norway, I find the aroma of Japanese natto – a fermented soybean product – quite pleasant. It has often made me question where exactly I fit in culturally. I guess this highlights the complexity of cultural identity and how our sensory experiences can shape our sense of belonging.

The concept of each culture having its own favourite smell contrasts with artistic endeavours aimed at establishing a universal favourite scent. Gayil Nalls, an interdisciplinary artist and theorist based in New York, has been a trailblazer in the field of olfactory art. Her visionary project, "World Sensorium" (1999–2000), sought to create a completely new *shared scent memory* by composing national scents from around the world. These scents were diffused in places where large crowds gathered, such as the millennium celebration in Times Square, New York. The aim was to forge a new collective memory in an era of globalization, where citizens of the present could recall their shared presence through a specific smell. Nalls' vision was to craft a global memory using an undisclosed formula, derived from population percentages, reflecting her exploration and definition of the "aesthetics of mass anatomy".

The installation resembled a shapeless sculpture, moulded by the people experiencing it. This ongoing work, termed a "social sculpture", continues to evolve as it is shared in international public events attended by large crowds. Through "World Sensorium", Nalls managed to transcend cultural boundaries and create a sensory experience that unites people across geographical and cultural divides.

I enjoy following the work of olfactory artists, as I often gain valuable insights that inform various aspects of my own work. For instance, the Japanese olfactory artist Maki Ueda provides fascinating revelations about how motherhood is perceived and constructed socio-culturally through certain smells. One of her installations explored the Japanese expression "A woman that stinks like Nukamiso", which refers to housewives who are perceived as unattractive because they are deeply embedded in family life: Nukamiso is a salted rice-bran paste used for making pickles, and it requires daily maintenance.

Traditionally, women who stayed at home would often handle this paste, causing their hands to absorb its smell. This expression highlights the cultural analogy: just as Nukamiso requires constant care, these women are seen as being absorbed in domestic duties to the point of losing their attractiveness, hence the derogatory expression.

However, as Ueda wrote in the accompanying brochure for the exhibition, this image might be outdated. Nowadays, Nukazuke (pickles made with Nukamiso) is often bought at supermarkets, and many women no longer know how to make it at home. This shift raises an interesting question about the evolving perception of motherhood. Perhaps those who smell like Nukazuke might come to be seen as attractive, as they represent mothers who spend time at home with their children – a rare and valued role given the increasing difficulty of affording preschool and kindergarten services across cultures. This changing context suggests a potential re-evaluation of traditional domestic smells and their associated cultural meanings.

It is an intriguing thought because smells that are too tightly connected to specific cultures can act as a discriminatory tool and divide cultures.

Social hierarchies and smell

Smells can be used to divide people into classes and social classes and there are several historical reviews showing how a focus on smell as a code for social segregation, can reveal discriminatory patterns in human history. Kapoor's (2021) examination delves deeply into the intricate dynamics of castes, shedding light on how this social practice has historically revolved around the "sensory management of bodies". Castes are social stratifications based on hereditary hierarchy, often characterized by rigid roles and occupations within a community. Castes have historically influenced various aspects of life, including marriage, occupation, and social interaction. Within caste systems, olfaction has been leveraged as a tool to establish and perpetuate hierarchies and inequalities. Critical scholars, often collaborating with artists, approach this subject from the margins, centring the experiences of marginalized groups. By focusing on these perspectives, they aim to unravel the complex patterns and power dynamics inherent within caste structures (Classen, 1992).

Victoria Henshaw's groundbreaking research on the urban smellscapes of the UK is the first of its kind to delve into the role of smell in contemporary experiences and perceptions of English towns and cities. Henshaw (2013) notes how smells associated with cultural diversity, such as "international food odours", are often labelled as "out of place" in xenophobic disputes over heritage.

As discussed in earlier chapters regarding methodology, the absence of objective and standardized measures for identifying specific smells tied to a location makes the olfactory biases especially tricky. We must avoid perpetuating past patterns and favouring smell cultures that align with those of the dominant group, and for that we need suitable methodologies and good measures. Otherwise, we might be systematically marginalizing historically underrepresented groups and over-representing the smells and olfactory practices that define the higher culture.

In my own research, I try to navigate this issue through the lens of my identity as a white woman from Norway who is curious about but very far away from fully understanding the smellscapes of, for example, Africa. For instance, my studies in Malawi and my travels to Rwanda have provided insights into the diverse olfactory cultures of these regions. They have also reminded me that the Western emphasis on visual and auditory senses is distinctly Western, and my upbringing, which regarded smell as a "lower sense", reflects a cultural heritage influenced by long-standing traditions. The notion of smell as a lower sense was, in my upbringing, part of the history classes where Aristotle and the Greek philosophers and Hellenic studies were central primary and secondary education. By acknowledging and embracing these cultural differences in how we perceive and value olfaction, we can work towards a more inclusive understanding of the role of smell in shaping our perceptions of others and their smells.

Industrialized versus non-industrialized societies

Poirier and Melin (2024) reviewed the literature that suggests that non-industrialized societies generally rely more on smells in their daily lives and have a richer vocabulary for olfactory experiences compared with industrialized societies. This difference is attributed to a mix of environmental, cultural, and possibly genetic factors. For instance, one study comparing neighbouring hunting and gathering societies with agricultural societies did not find significant differences in the number of functional olfactory receptor genes, implying that culture and physical environment might play a more significant role in olfactory differences among cultures. In addition, Poirier and Melin (2024) highlight that the cultural and genetic diversity present in modern human societies is likely reflected in their collective awareness and understanding of smells.

My journey to Rwanda served as a poignant reminder that what Western cultures often tout as recent discoveries actually have deep roots in African culture. For instance, aromatherapy, a practice widely associated with modern wellness movements, has been a longstanding tradition in the earliest civilizations of Africa.

Even Hippocrates, who is often regarded as the father of Western medicine, drew inspiration from ancient Egyptians and their technique of "enfleurage", which involved extracting oils from flowers for medicinal purposes. Similarly, figures like Pliny and Galen, whose works are seminal in Western natural history and medicine respectively, incorporated African herbs into their practices. Indeed, in many African countries, herbalism and its associated aroma knowledge were deeply ingrained in collective wisdom, rather than confined to isolated experts or master perfumers.

A discussion of industrialization's influences on olfactory history would not be complete without considering the significant environmental issues faced by the Global South countries. The global fragrance industry's demand for natural raw materials, such as essential oils and absolutes, has led to significant environmental concerns in African countries. These materials, often harvested manually, require substantial labour input, including the collection of plant parts (leaves or bark) by children in some cases. The popularity of certain scents, like cedarwood and frankincense, has resulted in the overharvesting of aromatic trees, particularly in countries like Ethiopia, Somalia, and Kenya.

Sustainability researchers have highlighted how frankincense, which has been traded on the global market for more than 5,000 years, is particularly vulnerable to overharvesting and eco-damaging practices. The frankincense substance, the resin of *Boswellia* trees, is popular across the world given its multiple purposes, from religious rituals as an ambient smell to medicinal properties (frankincense can be used to treat small wounds, and skin infection, and is thus very often used in Ayurvedic and Chinese traditional medicines).

The consequences of overharvesting Frankincense are twofold. First, it contributes to the establishment of monocultures in regions naturally abundant with these aromatic trees, disrupting local ecosystems. Second, excessive tapping of trees for their oils can directly harm their populations. Recent studies have highlighted the decline in frankincense tree populations due to overexploitation, with heavily tapped trees exhibiting low rates of seed germination compared with untouched trees. Weakened trees are also more susceptible to damage from natural disasters like storms and less resilient to drought conditions (see the Save Frankincense initiative: https://www.savefrankincense.org/).

As a strong advocate for sustainable practices in the fragrance industry, I endorse the synthetic production of scent ingredients that would otherwise be sourced from endangered trees. Additionally, when utilizing natural resources, awareness-raising initiatives, community mobilization and engagement are crucial for the responsible management and protection of these valuable botanical assets (Leminih & Teketay, 2003).

Cultural universals

One aspect where I find it appropriate to consider smell as a universal phenomenon across cultures is in terms of human responses, particularly regarding the emotions–thoughts distinction. This became clear to me while reading Andreas Keller's description of how humans react to smells compared with visual stimuli.

Keller illustrates that, when presented with a painting of dead bodies, we recognize it as a representation and do not react as strongly as when we encounter the smell of actual corpses. Even if we are informed that the smell is artificially created in a laboratory and not real, our reaction remains potent. As Keller aptly puts it, we respond to representations differently from how we would react to the thing they represent: "emotions are easily elicited by smells, but thoughts are much more easily elicited by visual stimuli" (Keller, 2014, p. 172). This underscores the unique power of smells to evoke immediate emotional responses, distinct from the cognitive engagement elicited by visual stimuli.

Another way to illustrate the universal cultural connection to smell is through the lens of childhood memories. It is fascinating how, when prompted, anyone can drift into a Proustian moment, vividly describing their childhood experiences based on the scents of different foods, places, people, objects, and events.

I've often used this exercise when discussing the importance of smell and memory with teachers and early childhood educators. It serves as a delightful introduction to the topic of smell and why I research it with children. Alongside the shared reference to childhood memories, often in the form of olfactory memories, there's frequently a collective recollection of a scented artifact that resonates with a particular generation. For instance, the teachers I interviewed in England reminisced about scented erasers, popular in the 1980s, infused with artificial smells like grapes or cola. These shared olfactory memories not only serve as excellent conversation starters for reminiscing but also foster group bonding and facilitate discussions about the significance of smell.

Bonding over olfactory memories is an activity that anyone can try with both adults and children. Here's how I do it: I distribute a sheet for collecting notes on olfactory memories. On this sheet, participants note down the name of the smell (often the source of the smell, such as food or herbs), the intensity of the smell on a scale of 1 to 5 (where 5 is the most intense), the pleasantness of the smell on a scale from 1 to 5 (with 5 being very pleasant and 1 very unpleasant), and volatility, which indicates how quickly the smell evaporates, again on a scale of 1 to 5 (with 5 being the least volatile and still lingering in the air). To stimulate different smells, there are multiple techniques; one can be a walk in the surroundings, while another, more controlled method, is to have a set of scents with you.

For instance, participants can experience a collection of essential oils one by one, noting down their impressions. They can first record their impressions alone, then swap the smells with the person next to them and discuss. This discussion can also take place in a larger group, with everyone reporting aloud to others. When working with children, I often use a selection of smells from a Montessori game, as these are already at concentrations safe for children to use. With children, I focus less on discussing memory and more on what the smell reminds them of and whether they can tell a story about it. In collaboration with teachers, we have encouraged children to bring from home specific objects that they wanted us to smell in the kindergarten and share with others. This was a great way to involve family cultures in the olfactory reflections, and to incorporate diverse perceptions of the same smell into our collective knowledge. Ultimately, such olfactory reflections enable us to explore new dimensions of our "olfactory heritage".

Olfactory heritage serves as a shared cultural element among various societies, extending beyond research to convey the significance of smells in defining a cultural community. These shared odours are intricately linked with significant customs, habits, prejudices, language, and communal spaces or environments. Preserving olfactory heritage involves passing down these aromatic traditions to future generations and I want to finish this chapter by highlighting the importance of incorporating this intentionality into early education.

Olfactory heritage

With Neema Mwenda Chinula, I conducted a research project involving twenty-five children and two teachers from two primary schools in semi-urban Malawi (Kucirkova & Chinula, 2023). We explored the olfactory experiences children had in these classrooms. Children were asked about their favourite smells and to draw a story that would contain the smells. The drawing method proved too limited for reporting on smells, as none of the children incorporated smells into their stories. Instead, they verbally shared their favourite smells with Neema and these ranged from food-related odours, such as "nsima" and "meat", to various plant-related smells, including "guava" and "masuku" (an indigenous tree with the scientific name Uapaca kirkiana). Interestingly, two children described their favourite smell as the scent of new clothes.

Neema also documented key odours in the classroom. These included the pleasant smell of freshly washed clothes and the unpleasant smell of unwashed clothes. Additional odours included the neutral smell of wet floors or wet soil inside the classroom, the teacher's perfume, and chalk dust. Unpleasant smells such as sweat and urine were also noted. The lack of ventilation was identified as a key factor contributing to the presence of unpleasant smells.

In a follow-up analysis (Kucirkova et al., 2023), we examined how agency is represented in the drawings of the forty-nine children who participated in the study. Our conclusion was that agency is far from an individual phenomenon. Instead, in the children's drawings, agency appeared as communal and highly context-dependent. While some children depicted what they, the characters in their drawings, or others liked to do, more often they illustrated various chores, such as sweeping the floor or cutting the grass, emphasizing their role in the family and community.

These stories reflected lived experiences within their communities, with literacies extending beyond books into communal narratives, aligning with the concept of artifactural living literacies as described by Pahl and Rowsell (2013). In this context, olfaction entered the stories through routes distinct from those in other cultures, such as Norway. The findings made us think of olfaction not necessarily residing in stories or drawings but rather in the lived culture as part of a country's olfactory heritage.

At present, UNESCO does not explicitly include smell in its definition of intangible cultural heritage, yet indirect references abound in areas such as food and culinary practices or folk medicine. Anthropologists dedicated to the studies of olfactory heritage describe these practices as essential for understanding how different cultures communicate and live their literacies. Olfactory heritage researchers also recognize the challenge I have emphasized throughout this book: the difficulty of capturing smell through reliable methodologies. Approached from the cultural perspective, the ephemerality of smell highlights the universal fascination with transience in human lives. In this sense, smell serves as both an intriguing characteristic and a reminder of human mortality, perhaps explaining its universal fascination across cultures and the inherent human desire to preserve cherished memories, such as those from childhood.

6 Anticipating olfactory education futures

In 1991, Linda Buck and Richard Axel made a groundbreaking discovery by cloning the receptors responsible for odorant discrimination (Buck & Axel, 1991). Their research unveiled a remarkable fact: approximately 3 per cent of our entire genome is dedicated to genes that detect various odours. Each of these genes produces a receptor specifically designed to detect an odour molecule. In recognition of their groundbreaking work, Buck and Axel were awarded the Nobel Prize in 2004.

It may seem unconventional that I address the role of genes towards the end of this book, but I actually find the study of the genetic origins of olfactory abilities highly relevant to the future prospects of olfaction in education, which I want to probe in this chapter.

Olfactory research with animals

When discussing genetics, comparisons with other species often arise, including olfactory research with dogs or mice. Rodents, like many other mammals, rely heavily on their sense of smell to navigate social interactions and parental care. These cues activating parental behaviour circuits involve various sensory stimuli, whereby the olfactory system, shows a high degree of adaptability in the context of parenthood. This suggests that olfaction is heavily involved in instinct-led and learned aspects of parental behaviour in mice. Researchers have identified the connection between atypical olfaction and therapeutic options for individuals diagnosed with autism spectrum disorder and also the association between olfactory receptor genes and autism (Dudas et al., 2024). This research helps us understand genetic models for human conditions such as autism spectrum disorder, although the actual application of findings needs much more research to be conclusive. Furthermore, most of what we know about rodent parenting

DOI: 10.4324/9781003482024-6

comes from studying a small group of domesticated species in labs. It is important to remember that lab conditions are different from animals' natural environments, which can affect how they use their senses and how they behave.

In addition to mice, dogs are often studied in olfactory research due to their remarkable ability to detect odours at concentrations nearly 100 million times lower than those detectable by humans. Evolutionary theory explains this phenomenon by suggesting a trade-off between smell and vision in animals: the better an animal's vision, the less acute its sense of smell needs to be, and vice versa. This trade-off implies that animals typically excel in either smell or vision, but not both simultaneously, as developing highly complex versions of both sensory systems would require significant biological resources. Dogs can detect smells that are undetectable to the human nose, including certain chemicals emitted by sick individuals. These smell detections by trained dogs can lead to early diagnoses of illnesses, often preceding the comprehensive medical evaluations typically required for diagnosis. This is where the term "dognoseis" comes from; it is used to describe a dog's ability to sniff out cancer in humans.

Various experiments highlight dogs' remarkable innate sense of smell. In the engaging Genius Dog Challenge research project, dogs recruited from owners who observed their pets distinguishing between toy names showcased impressive abilities. In one experiment by Dror et al. (2022), dogs were tasked to locate their favourite toys. When playing in both light and darkness, dogs attentively observed toy features, utilizing multiple senses. In darkness, they relied more on their olfactory sense, while in light, their visual sense took precedence. Just imagine if humans could do the same!

These recent discoveries regarding the workings of the brain and olfaction primarily stem from studies involving mice and dogs, with findings extrapolated to humans due to the assumed similarity in function. Similar to how butterflies perceive the world through varying light ranges, dogs navigate their environment primarily through their sense of smell. As humans, we often overlook the diverse ways in which different species interact with our shared environment. And yet, the sensory cues crucial to our experiences may vastly differ from those of other species coexisting on our planet.

In considering the future of our approach to smell, I would like us to reflect on humanity and our relationship with this sense. To delve into this topic, I've structured the remainder of this chapter around two fundamental dimensions of reality: time and space. By exploring how humans perceive smell across different temporal and spatial contexts, I hope to provide some insight into the evolving significance of olfaction in our lives and its potential implications for the future.

Time

In our modern lives, time is a structured concept, often dictated by work schedules, school routines, and daily habits. But what if our perception of time were influenced by smell? Unlike concrete entities, both time and smell possess abstract qualities that shape our experiences. When confronted with unpleasant odours, our routines are interrupted: for example, if, while reading this book with the window open, the sewage in the neighbouring building starts leaking, and an unpleasant smell starts drifting in from the street, your reading time will be disrupted. This inherent ability of odours to disrupt time raises an intriguing question: what if we organized our days according to different olfactory cues?

If we consider the role of olfactory memories, it becomes evident that smell can serve as a powerful trigger for mental time travel. Unlike semantic memories, which are based on factual knowledge, episodic memories are constructed through a blend of sensory information. These memories are stored in specialized brain systems and linked together through associative networks. Retrieving such memories can occur through various stimuli, whether visual, auditory, or olfactory, as the brain reactivates patterns of features associated with past experiences. Thus, the relationship between time and smell offers a fascinating avenue for exploring how our perceptions of time are intertwined with sensory experiences.

In the previous chapter, I explored the concept of olfactory heritage, which underscores how certain collective memories are not only tied to specific places but also to distinct eras. Both places and eras carry unique olfactory cues that evoke a sense of time and place, anchoring individuals to their biographical past and fostering a connection to memory. Building on this idea, the potential of olfaction for revisiting the past self involves constructing one's perception of the world through smell. This notion is supported by research conducted by Waskul et al. (2009), who found that participants who kept a diary based on various smells viewed it as a means of preserving stability in the past and consolidating their identity:

> Human beings employ a number of strategies in their attempt to maintain a stable self over time. Active reminiscing can be one such strategy. And reminiscences and nostalgia may seamlessly

> flow from the "placing" of a specific aroma, that is, from the incorporation of memory onto flesh and self (Connerton 1989; Schwaiger 2008). We are not saying "you are what you smell," but we are saying that those things that we associate with particular smells can be highly relevant to the processes of sensuous self construction, (re)construction, and self identity.
>
> (Waskul et al., 2009, p. 19)

Indeed, linking events to memory goes beyond merely facilitating group discussion; it plays a vital role in constructing a cohesive identity. This process is essential not only for the mental well-being of individuals but also for fostering group identity and bonding.

It is no wonder that some of the oldest rituals revolve around food, as the chemosenses of taste and smell are intricately intertwined with the experience of eating and shared time. These rituals serve as powerful tools for connecting individuals to their history and reinforcing a sense of belonging within the group.

When time hurts

The connection between smell and memory also has a dark side: the potential to trigger traumatic experiences. For war survivors, the smell of dust after a city bombing or the perfume of a perpetrator can bring back intense and distressing memories. Clinicians in modern post-traumatic stress disorder (PTSD) treatment often utilize odour therapy with systematic desensitization because scents are highly effective memory cues, evoking strong emotions. Scents uniquely access and activate memories, making them powerful triggers for traumatic recollections, highlighting the intricate relationship between smell and memory and their ability to unlock past experiences, both positive and painful (Herz, 2009).

Geddes (2022) studied parents who had had their children taken for fostering or adoption, noting how in the narratives of these parents, smell was essential for comforting them and triggering memories of the child. Geddes describes in her research how one of the participants, called Ruby, found solace in sleeping in her daughter's bed after her two eldest children were adopted, as it allowed her to feel close to her daughter. Similarly, another participant, called Louise, recalled that she would frequently smell her sons' clothing while they were in foster care and after they were adopted. For these participants, touching and smelling their children's clothes served as a way to momentarily bridge the separation between mother and child, providing them with a sensory memory of their child's smell and feel before their adoption. These interactions with artifacts had the power to transcend time, offering a sense of connection beyond the physical absence of their children.

One way therapists have been utilizing research findings on the olfaction–time connection is through the evidence from bereavement studies, suggesting that touching and smelling items belonging to lost loved ones can offer comfort to the bereaved and evoke a sense of the deceased's continuing presence. It is essential that professionals are involved in olfactory therapies as imagined but not real aromas (the so-called Phantom aromas) can be easily triggered and induce also Phantom memories.

Another way of using olfaction in therapy is through olfactory glimmers. While the effectiveness of olfactory glimmers is not yet clear, I have encountered this practice being used quite frequently with children who have special needs. A glimmer refers to a delightful sensory experience that fills someone with intense joy. A glimmer is thus in direct contrast with a trigger, which is perceived as threatening or unsafe. In this context, olfactory glimmers are often utilized, such as the smell of a favourite food or the calming aroma of lavender, to provide comfort and pleasure.

Bringing odours intentionally and carefully into experiences is crucial in both research and practice and this applies not only in exploring our identities across the past but also our identities across space.

Space

Part of our project in Norway was an intentionally designed odour-based space for children, such as an exhibition at the local museum featuring boxes with scents accompanying stories, as well as in libraries. I've encouraged teachers to adopt similar approaches in the classroom, organizing the rooms and resources in kindergartens not by words or colours, but by scents. While natural smells exist and don't require additional inducement, the aim is to draw attention and intentionally enhance our everyday environments using smells. It is this intentionality that I would like to bring to the discussion of future resources and spaces enhanced with olfaction.

Many commercial producers are incorporating smell into their products and resources for everyday use. While most current digital learning platforms for children prioritize visual and auditory senses, a new generation of technologies focuses on the interplay of connected senses. The advances in generative AI models are particularly fast. While writing this book, Meta announced the ImageBind model, which combines text, audio, visual, movement, thermal, and depth data. This project is still in the research phase, but it gives us a glimpse into how future AI models might create content that appeals to multiple senses. ImageBind is the first model to bring together six different kinds of information in one place. These include visual data (like images and videos), thermal data (like heat images), text, audio, depth details, and something really interesting – data about movement in space captured by a device called an inertial measuring unit (IMU). You can find IMUs in phones and smartwatches, where they're used for various tasks, like switching a phone's screen orientation or tracking different types of physical activity (Vincent, 2023). OpenAI and Google are sure to follow with their models, as it is an appealing idea that future AI systems will be able to cross-reference this data in the same way that current AI systems do for text inputs. Ultimately, the technologists behind these inventions aim to create a fully immersive virtual reality where experiences can be generated on command in all senses. With these advancements, our spatial perception can thus be artificially generated to engage all senses.

In a future driven by generative artificial intelligence rather than human agency and natural sensory experiences, it is crucial to strengthen the call for prioritizing our senses, including smell, in education. We must ensure that our reliance on technology does not further undermine our connection to our sensory faculties but rather reinforces and enhances them.

Rachel Herz, a scent psychologist, highlighted in her book, *The Scent of Desire*, that humans struggle to differentiate between real fragrances and their synthetic counterparts. This could be attributed to factors such as greater familiarity with synthetic versions or the heightened concentration of artificial scents. This suggests a departure from, rather than a return to, our senses' innate abilities.

Indeed, historic analyses suggest that the sense of smell appears to have atrophied or become less developed and complex (Herz, 2009). The deterioration is possibly due to a combination of factors, including a reduced emphasis on its development, less research on it compared with other senses, and a modern environment saturated with intense stimuli. In today's world, our senses seem to crave increasingly intense input, whether it be fast-paced visuals, louder music, or more potent fragrances. This trend raises concerns that we may be losing the ability to perceive nuances and subtle scents in sophisticated ways.

Building upon the social justice themes discussed in Chapter 2, I want to critically examine how children's agency is impacted by such technology-driven experiences that engage multiple senses. Many teachers and parents I speak to highlight the ethical concerns surrounding experiences crafted by adults for children with minimal input from the children themselves, as well as the heightened level of engagement that arises when all senses are involved. These emerging technological trends, coupled with limited agency, underscore the importance of involving multiple stakeholders, including researchers, educators, publishers, children's book authors, and human–computer interaction designers, in deliberating the appropriate and purposeful integration of smell in learning environments. Ultimately, these efforts are envisioned as essential components of fostering socially just educational futures in the twenty-first century.

Future olfactory education

It is puzzling to me that, despite the fundamental importance of smell, curriculum design pays so little attention to this sense. Unlike other senses, taste and smell cannot be easily ignored or suppressed because they are essential for survival. While our eyes can be diverted or deceived, our noses are always engaged. McBride and Nolan (2017) put it precisely: "it is curious that we do not place a greater premium on teaching children empirical skills of detecting, identifying, and discriminating between odours as a form of physical knowledge".

Will we start teaching children the "alphabet of smells", or what Tolaas refers to as the "alphabet of the nose", preparing them to become future "nasalnauts"?

Providing direct curriculum ideas is complicated because, as explained, we are developing methodologies for studying olfaction as we speak, and the knowledge on how children respond to various smells is limited. Another factor against direct application is that many environmental odours are quickly disappearing because of biodiversity loss, further challenging recommendations for stable learning curricula. Nevertheless, there are ways to include children in the process and maintain a collective orientation rather than let technological innovations drive the developments.

Children could be involved not only through small literacy activities and scented resources but also through larger community-oriented installations. Perhaps no one is more innovative in this space than the contemporary olfactory French artist Pierre Bénard. Bénard is known for perfuming streets and open-air concerts and creating unusual installations that attribute smells to imaginary beings such as ghosts. The artist's inspiration comes from Rimmel, the perfume house, which, in the 1850s during the performance of Chrysabella, released the odour of a rose into the theatre audience. This inspired Bénard to use smell to create ambience and, today, Bénard works with molecules that can be visualized and integrated into music. In Toulouse, he created scented bricks in walls, encouraging children to participate through school by finding and smelling these bricks. Unlike literacy scholars and how we approached olfaction in our work, Bénard starts with the odour, the perfume. Each perfume has a personality, guiding him to various installations and concerts. He strongly incorporates movement into his art, connecting it to air in dance, which allows for the drifting and wafting of smells. He dreams of choreographers who would be inspired to create dances for odours. As odours increasingly appear in theatres and children frequently visit these venues, I dream of such olfactory installations to become more common in children's art experiences.

As futurists delve into the realm of space exploration, I am captivated by the notion that smell may possess its own unique characteristics, including an entirely unexplored array of olfactospaces, beyond Earth. Astronauts often struggle to describe the aroma of space when they return to Earth, yet they distinctly recall its presence. To me, this represents a fascinating conundrum, particularly due to the effects of weightlessness in space. Astronauts often report a loss of taste and smell while in orbit, as the absence of gravity prevents molecules from becoming volatile. Consequently, the olfactory experience in space is markedly different, if not absent altogether, as these molecules are unable to interact with the nasal receptors in the same manner as they do on Earth (Ackerman, 1991). With space travel being more frequent in the future, how will this affect our relationship with the sense of smell?

I don't hold the crystal ball of future projection, but I did play with some predictions for an article I wrote for Wired in 2022. In it, I foresaw the rise of olfactory broadcasters and predicted that olfactory devices would become as mainstream as TVs and radios. The evolution, I noted, has progressed from static images to dynamic, fast-paced visuals. Similarly, in music, we transitioned from locally produced tunes to those broadcast over radio, offered in various intensities. Now, with touch, we have virtual transmitters like kissengers. However, in the realm of fragrances, while we can select the intensity, we lack the means to transmit it. This gap suggests a need for devices akin to radios for smells.

Could we also envision the development of spaces akin to symphony halls, designed to isolate olfaction from urban smells? Picture olfactory museum exhibitions where visitors come solely to experience scents, mirroring the way people attend concerts solely for the music. And instead of using microscopes, imagine a nose-centric experience that extends the sense of smell.

Regardless of what the immediate future holds, I hope that this book has persuaded you that it is worth changing both education and the wider culture to become more attuned and attentive to the sense of smell. Just as we teach children the alphabet to engage with literature, musical notes to enjoy music, and shapes and colours for visual art appreciation, it is equally important to introduce olfactory notes into education. This will enable children to appreciate olfactory art and understand the significance of smell in their lives. To support this process, I have developed several online accompanying resources with suggested activities for incorporating smell into early education. These activities are intended for anyone who interacts with children: teachers, practitioners, curators of exhibitions, public spaces such as galleries and museums, architects designing playgrounds and kindergartens, librarians preparing reading sessions for children, as well as publishers of books and developers of apps and digital games. While smell may have been neglected in the past, I urge you to now prioritize it in your endeavours. It is high time we give olfaction the space that it deserves.

References

Ackerman, D. (1991). *A natural history of the senses.* Vintage.

Amoore, J. E. (1952). Stereochemical specificities of human olfactory receptors. *Perfumery and Essential Oil Record*, 43, 321–323.

Amoore, J. E. (1963). Stereochemical theory of olfaction. *Nature*, 271–272. doi:10.1038/198271a0.

Banes, S. (2001). Olfactory performances. *TDR/The Drama Review*, 45(1), 68–76. https://www.muse.jhu.edu/article/33046.

Biswas, T. (2021). Who needs sensory education? *Studies in Philosophy and Education*, 40(3), 287–302.

Block, E., Jang, S., Matsunami, H., Batista, V. S., & Zhuang, H. (2015). Reply to Turin et al.: Vibrational theory of olfaction is implausible. *Proceedings of the National Academy of Sciences*, 112(25), E3155–E3155.

Bodnar, A., Corbett, R., & Nekrasovski, D. (2004, October). AROMA: Ambient awareness through olfaction in a messaging application. In *Proceedings of the 6th international conference on Multimodal interfaces* (pp. 183–190). Association for Computing Machinery.

Brämerson, A., Johansson, L., Ek, L., Nordin, S., & Bende, M. (2004). Prevalence of olfactory dysfunction: the Skövde population-based study. *The Laryngoscope*, 114(4), 733–737.

Bray, P. M. (2013). Forgetting the madeleine: Proust and the neurosciences. *Progress in Brain Research*, 205, 41–53.

Brod, G., Kucirkova, N., Shepherd, J., Jolles, D., & Molenaar, I. (2023). Agency in educational technology: Interdisciplinary perspectives and implications for learning design. *Educational Psychology Review*, 35(1), 25.

Brooks, J. (2020). Scratch & sniff book open dataset. https://jasbrooks.net/snsdataset2020.

Buck, L., & Axel, R. (1991). A novel multigene family may encode odorant receptors: A molecular basis for odor recognition. *Cell*, 65(1), 175–187.

Burnett, C., Davies, J., Merchant, G., & Rowsell, J. (2014a). New literacies around the globe. *Policy and pedagogy.* Routledge.

Burnett, C., Merchant, G., Pahl, K., & Rowsell, J. (2014b). The (im) materiality of literacy: The significance of subjectivity to new literacies research. *Discourse: Studies in the Cultural Politics of Education*, 35(1), 90–103.

Burr, C. (2002). *The emperor of scent: A true story of perfume and obsession*. Random House.

Bushdid, C., Magnasco, M. O., Vosshall, L. B., & Keller, A. (2014). Humans can discriminate more than 1 trillion olfactory stimuli. *Science*, 343(6177), 1370–1372.

Ceccarelli, I., Lariviere, W. R., Fiorenzani, P., Sacerdote, P., & Aloisi, A. M. (2004). Effects of long-term exposure of lemon essential oil odor on behavioral, hormonal and neuronal parameters in male and female rats. *Brain Research*, 1001(1–2), 78–86.

Chanel.com (n.d.). Fragrance No. 5. *Chanel* website. https://www.chanel.com/gb/fragrance/women/c/7x1x1x30/n5/.

Classen, C. (1992). The odor of the other: olfactory symbolism and cultural categories. *Ethos*, 20(2), 133–166.

Classen, C. (1993). *Worlds of senses: Exploring the senses in history and across cultures*. New York: Routledge.

Comber, B. (2015). *Literacy, place, and pedagogies of possibility*. New York: Routledge.

Cope, B., & Kalantzis, M. (Eds.). (2000). *Multiliteracies: Literacy learning and the design of social futures*. Psychology Press.

Cowan, K. (2020). Tracing the ephemeral: Mapping young children's running games. *Designs for Learning*, 12(1), 81–93.

Crisinel, A. -S., & Spence, C. (2009). Implicit association between basic tastes and pitch. *Neuroscience Letters*, 464(1), 39–42.

Crisinel, A. -S., & Spence, C. (2012). A fruity note: Crossmodal associations between odors and musical notes. *Chemical Senses*, 37(2), 151–158.

Croy, I., Frackowiak, T., Hummel, T., & Sorokowska, A. (2017). Babies smell wonderful to their parents, teenagers do not: An exploratory questionnaire study on children's age and personal odor ratings in a polish sample. *Chemosensory Perception*, 10, 81–87.

Damon, F., Mezrai, N., Magnier, L., Leleu, A., Durand, K., & Schaal, B. (2021). Olfaction in the multisensory processing of faces: A narrative review of the influence of human body odors. *Frontiers in Psychology*, 12, 750944.

Diaconu, M. (2022). Being and making the olfactory self. Lessons from contemporary artistic practices. In Di Stefano, N., & Russo, M. T. (Eds.), *Olfaction: An interdisciplinary perspective from philosophy to life sciences* (pp. 55–73). Springer.

Dror, S., Sommese, A., Miklósi, Á., Temesi, A., & Fugazza, C. (2022). Multisensory mental representation of objects in typical and Gifted Word Learner dogs. *Animal Cognition*, 25(6), 1557–1566.

Dudas, A., Nakahara, T. S., Pellissier, L. P., & Chamero, P. (2024). Parenting behaviors in mice: Olfactory mechanisms and features in models of autism spectrum disorders. *Neuroscience & Biobehavioral Reviews*, 105686.

Epple, G., & Herz, R. S. (1999). Ambient odors associated to failure influence cognitive performance in children. *Developmental Psychobiology*, 35, 103–107.

Faas, A. E., Spontón, E. D., Moya, P. R., & Molina, J. C. (2000). Differential responsiveness to alcohol odor in human neonates: Efects of maternal consumption during gestation. *Alcohol*, 22(1), 7–17.

Fletcher, J. (1998). *Oils and perfumes of ancient Egypt*. British Museum Press.

Geddes, E. (2022). "Some days it's like she has died." A qualitative exploration of first mothers' utilisation of artefacts associated with now-adopted children in coping with grief and loss. *Qualitative Social Work*, 21(5), 811–832.

Gellrich, J., Stetzler, C., Oleszkiewicz, A., Hummel, T., & Schriever, V. A. (2017). Olfactory threshold and odor discrimination ability in children – evaluation of a modified "Sniffin'Sticks" test. *Scientific Reports*, 7(1), 1928.

Gilbert, A. (2008). *What the nose knows: The science of scent in everyday life*. CreateSpace Independent Publishing Platform.

Gögele, M., Emmert, D., Fuchsberger, C., & Frasnelli, J. (2024). Factors influencing olfactory function in an adult general population sample: the CHRIS study. *Chemical Senses*, 49, bjae011.

Heller, M. A., & Gentaz, E. (2014). *Psychology of touch and blindness*. Psychology Press.

Henrich, J., Heine, S. J., & Norenzayan, A. (2010). Beyond WEIRD: Towards a broad-based behavioral science. *Behavioral and Brain Sciences*, 33(2–3), 111.

Henshaw, V. (2013). *Urban smellscapes: Understanding and designing city smell environments*. London: Routledge.

Hepper, P. G. (1995). Human fetal "olfactory" learning. *International Journal of Prenatal and Perinatal Psychology and Medicine*, 7(2), 147–151.

Herz, R. (2009). *The scent of desire: Discovering our enigmatic sense of smell*. Harper Collins.

Herz, R. S., & Cupchik, G. C. (1995). The emotional distinctiveness of odor-evoked memories. *Chemical Senses*, 20(5), 517–528.

Heydon, R., & Rowsell, J. (2015). Phenomenology and literacy studies. In *The Routledge handbook of literacy studies* (pp. 454–471). Routledge.

Hoehn, R. D., Nichols, D. E., Neven, H., & Kais, S. (2018). Status of the vibrational theory of olfaction. *Frontiers in Physics*, 6, 25.

Howes, D. (2010). *Sensual relations: Engaging the senses in culture and social theory*. University of Michigan Press.

Howes, D. (2021). Introduction: Empires of the senses. In *Empire of the Senses* (pp. 1–17). Routledge.

Howes, D. (2024). *Sensorium: Contextualizing the senses and cognition in history and across cultures*. Cambridge University Press.

Howes, D., & Classen, C. (2013). *Ways of sensing: Understanding the senses in society*. Routledge.

Hummel, T., Sekinger, B., Wolf, S. R., Pauli, E., & Kobal, G. (1997). 'Sniffin' sticks': Olfactory performance assessed by the combined testing of odor identification, odor discrimination and olfactory threshold. *Chemical Senses*, 22(1), 39–52.

Itenge, H., Muashekele, C., Chamunorwa, M. B., Winschiers-Theophilus, H., Brereton, M., & Soro, A. (2022). Design and evaluation of a social and embodied multiplayer reading game to engage primary school learners in Namibia. *British Journal of Educational Technology*, 53(6), 1571–1590.

Jacquot, M., Noel, F., Velasco, C., & Spence, C. (2016). On the colours of odours. *Chemosensory Perception*, 9, 79–93.

Kapoor, S. (2021). The smells of caste–body, self and politics. In Di Stefano, N. & Russo, M. T. (Eds.), *Olfaction: An interdisciplinary perspective from philosophy to life sciences* (pp. 21–34). Springer International Publishing.

Karan, N. B. (2019). Influence of lavender oil inhalation on vital signs and anxiety: A randomized clinical trial. *Physiology & Behavior*, 211, 112676.

Keller, A. (2014). The scented museum. In Levent, N., & Pascual-Leone, A. (Eds.), *The multisensory museum: Cross-disciplinary perspectives on touch, sound, smell, memory and space*, 167–176. Rowman & Littlefield.

Klatzky, R. L., Lederman, S. J., & Metzger, V. A. (1985). Identifying objects by touch: An expert system. *Perception & Psychophysics*, 37(4), 299–302. doi:10.3758/bf03211351.

Klatzky, R. L., Loomis, J. M., Lederman, S. J., Wake, H., & Fujita, N. (1993). Haptic identification of objects and their depictions. *Perception &Psychophysics*, 54(2), 170–178. doi:10.3758/bf03211752.

Knasko, S. C. (1995). Pleasant odors and congruency: Effects on approach behavior. *Chemical Senses*, 20(5), 479–487.

Koblet, O., & Purves, R. S. (2020). From online texts to Landscape Character Assessment: Collecting and analysing first-person landscape perception computationally. *Landscape and Urban Planning*, 197, 103757.

Kucirkova, N. (2023). Children's wayfaring experiences at an olfaction-enhanced Three Little Pigs story exhibition. *Museum and Society*, 21(3), 1–21.

Kucirkova, N. I. (2024). Fostering children's agency in their learning futures: Exploring the synergy of generative AI and sensory learning. *First Monday*.

Kucirkova, N., & Jensen, I. B. (2024). Parent–child shared reading of scratch-and-sniff books: The communicative affordance of olfaction. *European Early Childhood Education Research Journal*, 32(2), 297–310.

Kucirkova, N., & Kamola, M. (2022). Children's stories and multisensory engagement: Insights from a cultural probes study. *International Journal of Educational Research*, 114, 101995.

Kucirkova, N., & Mwenda Chinula, N. (2023). Olfactoscapes in Malawi: Exploring the smells children like and are exposed to in semi-urban classrooms. *Childhood*, 30(4), 451–470.

Kucirkova, N. I., & Tosun, S. (2023). Children's olfactory picturebooks: Charting new trends in early childhood education. *Early Childhood Education Journal*, 1–10.

Kucirkova, N., Rodriguez-Leon, L., & Chinula, N. M. (2023). Rethinking agency in literacies: Malawian children's and teachers' perspectives. *International Journal of Early Years Education*, 1–21.

Kucirkova, N. I., Campbell, J. A., Stangeland, E. B., & Hoel, T. (2023). The importance of sensorial and spatial aspects in family reading at home: Insights from a national survey in Norway. *International Journal of Educational Research Open*, 4, 100227.

Leminih, M., & Teketay, D. (2003). Frankincense and myrrh resources of Ethiopia: I distribution, production, opportunities for dryland development and research needs. *SINET: Ethiopian Journal of Science*, 26(1), 63–72.

Lenters, K. (2016). Riding the lines and overwriting in the margins: Affect and multimodal literacy practices. *Journal of Literacy Research*, 48(3), 280–316.

Loewer, A. (2006). Improving learner performance through olfactory intervention. *Annual Proceedings – Dallas*, 1, 255–262.

Løkken, I. M., Campbell, J. A., Kucirkova, N. I., & Dale, P. (2023). Experiment protocol: Exploring the sense of smell in digital book reading. *International Journal of Educational Research Open*, 5, 100285.

Majid, A. (2021). Human olfaction at the intersection of language, culture, and biology. *Trends in Cognitive Sciences*, 25(2), 111–123.

Mallet, P., & Schaal, B. (1998). Rating and recognition of peers' personal odors by 9-year-old children: An exploratory study. *The Journal of General Psychology*, 125(1), 47–64.

Martinec Nováková, L., & Havlíček, J. (2020). Time, age, gender, and test practice effects on children's olfactory performance: A two-year longitudinal study. *Chemosensory Perception*, 13(1), 19–36.

Martinec Nováková, L., Fialová, J., & Havlíček, J. (2018). Effects of diversity in olfactory environment on children's sense of smell. *Scientific Reports*, 8(1), 2937.

McBride, M., & Nolan, J. (2017). Situating olfactory literacies. An intersensory pedagogy by design, In Henshaw, V., McLean, K., Medway, D., Perkins, C., & Warnaby, G. (Eds.), *Designing with smell: Practices, techniques and challenges.* Routledge.

McKee, L. L., & Heydon, R. M. (2015). Orchestrating literacies: Print literacy learning opportunities within multimodal intergenerational ensembles. *Journal of Early Childhood Literacy*, 15(2), 227–255.

McLean, K., Perkins, C (2020). Smell walking and mapping. In Hall, S., & Holmes, H. (Eds.), *Mundane methods: Methodological innovations for exploring the everyday.* Manchester University Press.

Merchant, S. (2011). The body and the senses: Visual methods, videography and the submarine sensorium. *Body & Society*, 17(1), 53–72.

Mills, K. A. (2015). *Literacy theories for the digital age: Social, critical, multimodal, spatial, material and sensory lenses* (vol. 45). Multilingual Matters.

Mills, K. A., Unsworth, L., & Scholes, L. (2022). *Literacy for digital futures: Mind, body, text*. Routledge.

Mohammed, S., Ayragari, M. & Xie, L (2021). The life cycle of Chanel no5. *Design Life-Cycle* website: http://www.designlife-cycle.com/new-page-76.

Mullol, J., Alobid, I., Mariño-Sánchez, F., Izquierdo-Domínguez, A., Marin, C., Klimek, L., … & Liu, Z. (2020). The loss of smell and taste in the COVID-19 outbreak: A tale of many countries. *Current Allergy and Asthma Reports*, 20, 1–5.

Nikora, A. (2020). *Application of olfactory stimuli in a children's house Montessori classroom*. Master's thesis submitted at the University of Wisconsin.

Nováková, L., Varella Valentova, J., & Havlíček, J. (2014). Engagement in olfaction-related activities is associated with the ability of odor identification and odor awareness. *Chemosensory Perception*, 7, 56–67.

Owsienko, D., Loos, K., & Croy, I. (2024a). Unraveling the differences in chemical composition of children's body odor. *Nature Communication*, Available from: https://communities.springernature.com/posts/unraveling-the-differences-in-chemical-composition-of-children-s-body-odor.

Owsienko, D., Goppelt, L., Hierl, K., Schäfer, L., Croy, I., & Loos, H. M. (2024b). Body odor samples from infants and post-pubertal children differ in their volatile profiles. *Communications Chemistry*, 7(1), 1–10.

Pahl, K., & Rowsell, J. (2013). Artifactual literacies. In Albers, P., Holbrook, T., & Flint, A. (Eds.), *New methods of literacy research* (pp. 163–176). Routledge.

Pahl, K., & Rowsell, J. (2020). *Living literacies: Literacy for social change*. MIT Press.

Parker, M., Spennemann, D. H., & Bond, J. (2024). Methodologies for smellwalks and scentwalks – a critical review. *Chemical Senses*, bjae005.

Pierzchajlo, S., Jernsäther, T., Fontana, L., Almeida, R., & Olofsson, J. K. (2024). Olfactory categorization is shaped by a transmodal cortical network for evaluating perceptual predictions. *Journal of Neuroscience*, 44(22): e1232232024.

Poirier, A. C., & Melin, A. D. (2024). Smell throughout the life course. *Evolutionary Anthropology: Issues, News, and Reviews*, e22030.

Pool, S., Rowsell, J., & Sun, Y. (2023). Towards literacies of immanence: Getting closer to sensory multimodal perspectives on research. *Multimodality & Society*, 3(2), 130–149.

Rahayel, S., Frasnelli, J., & Joubert, S. (2012). The effect of Alzheimer's disease and Parkinson's disease on olfaction: a meta-analysis. *Behavioural Brain Research*, 231(1), 60–74.

Rastogi, S. C., Johansen, J. D., Menné, T., Frosch, P., Bruze, M., Andersen, K. E., … & White, I. R. (1999). Contents of fragrance allergens in children's cosmetics and cosmetic-toys. *Contact Dermatitis*, 41(2), 84–88.

Ravia, A., Snitz, K., Honigstein, D., Finkel, M., Zirler, R., Perl, O., & Sobel, N. (2020). A measure of smell enables the creation of olfactory metamers. *Nature*, 588(7836), 118–123.

Saxton, T. K., Martinec Nováková, L., Jash, R., Šandová, A., Plotěná, D., & Havlíček, J. (2014). Sex differences in olfactory behavior in Namibian and Czech children. *Chemosensory Perception*, 7(3), 117–125.

Schaal, B. (1988). Olfaction in infants and children: Developmental and functional perspectives. *Chemical Senses*, 13(2), 145–190.

Sefton-Green, J., Marsh, J., Erstad, O., & Flewitt, R. (2016). Establishing a research agenda for the digital literacy practices of young children. A White Paper for *COST Action* IS1410.

Sela, L., & Sobel, N. (2010). Human olfaction: A constant state of change-blindness. *Experimental Brain Research*, 205(1), 13–29.

Sheppard-Hanger, S., & Hanger, N. (2015). The importance of safety when using aromatherapy. *International Journal of Childbirth Education*, 30, 42–47.

Shiner, L. (2020). *Art scents: Exploring the aesthetics of smell and the olfactory arts.* Oxford University Press.

Sorokowski, P., Sorokowska, A., Misiak, M., & Roberts, S. C. (2023). Developmental changes in food and non-food odor importance – Data from Scotland and Pakistan. *Food Quality and Preference*, 111, 104963.

Speed, L. J., Croijmans, I., Dolscheid, S., & Majid, A. (2021). Crossmodal associations with olfactory, auditory, and tactile stimuli in children and adults. *i-Perception*, 12(6), doi:10.1177%2F20416695211048513.

Spence, C. (2011). Crossmodal correspondences: A tutorial review. *Attention, Perception, & Psychophysics*, 73, 971–995.

Spence, C. (2020). Using ambient scent to enhance well-being in the multi-sensory built environment. *Frontiers in Psychology*, 11, 598859.

Spence, C. (2022). Experimental atmospherics: a multi-sensory perspective. *Qualitative Market Research: An International Journal*, 25(5), 662–673.

Spence, C., Kucirkova, N., Campbell, J., Gao, Y., & Brooks, J. (2024). Narrative historical review of scratch-and-sniff books and their key storytelling features. *i-Perception*, 15(3), 20416695241257566.

Stratton, J. M., & Wright, S. (1991). *On the way to literacy: Early experiences for young visually impaired children.* American Printing House for the Blind.

Synnott, A. (1993). *The body social: Symbolism, self and society.* Routledge.

Torske, A., Koch, K., Eickhoff, S., & Freiherr, J. (2022). Localizing the human brain response to olfactory stimulation: A meta-analytic approach. *Neuroscience & Biobehavioral Reviews*, 134, 104512.

Tremblay, C., Serrano, G. E., Intorcia, A. J., Sue, L. I., Wilson, J. R., Adler, C. H., … & Beach, T. G. (2022). Effect of olfactory bulb pathology on olfactory function in normal aging. *Brain Pathology*, 32(5), e13075.

Turin, L. (1996). A spectroscopic mechanism for primary olfactory reception. *Chemical Senses*, 21(6), 773–791.

Tyagi, P., Bansal, S., Sharma, A., Tiwary, U. S., & Varadwaj, P. K. (2024). Differences in olfactory functioning: The role of personality and gender. *Journal of Sensory Studies*, 39(2), e12907.

Ueda, M. (2012). OLFACTOSCAPE – Lab for the Unstable Media. *v2.nl*. https://www.v2.nl/works/olfactoscape.

Vance, D. E., Del Bene, V. A., Kamath, V., Frank, J. S., Billings, R., Cho, D. Y., … & Fazeli, P. L. (2024). Does olfactory training improve brain function and cognition? A systematic review. *Neuropsychology Review*, 34(1), 155–191.

Verbeek, C., & Van Campen, C. (2013). Inhaling memories: Smell and taste memories in art, science, and practice. *The Senses and Society*, 8(2), 133–148.

Vincent, J. (2023). Meta open-sources multisensory AI model that combines six types of data. *The Verge*, https://www.theverge.com/2023/5/9/23716558/meta-imagebind-open-source-multisensory-modal-ai-model-research.

Ward, J. (2013). Synesthesia. *Annual Review of Psychology*, 64(1), 49–75.

Waskul, D. D., Vannini, P., & Wilson, J. (2009). The aroma of recollection: Olfaction, nostalgia, and the shaping of the sensuous self. *The Senses and Society*, 4(1), 5–22.

Zhao, S., & Unsworth, L. (2016). Touch design and narrative interpretation: A social semiotic approach to picture book apps. In Kucirkova, N. & Falloon, G. (Eds.), *Apps, technology and younger learners* (pp. 109–121). Routledge.

Index

Printed in the United States
by Baker & Taylor Publisher Services